· ACING THE ·

ACT

An Elite Tutor's Guide To Tricky
Questions and Secret Strategies
That Make A Big Difference

ELIZABETH KING

D0348469

TEN SPEED PRESS
Berkeley

All rights reserved.
Published in the United States by Ten Speed Press,
an imprint of the Crown Publishing Group, a division
of Random House LLC, a Penguin Random House
Company, New York.
www.crownpublishing.com
www.tenspeed.com

Ten Speed Press and the Ten Speed Press colophon are registered
trademarks of Random House LLC.

Library of Congress Cataloging-in-Publication Data

King, Elizabeth.
Acing the ACT : an elite tutor's guide to trick(y) questions and
secret little strategies that make a big difference / Elizabeth King.
    pages cm
Includes bibliographical references and index.
1. ACT Assessment—Study guides. I. Title.
LB2353.48.K55 2015
378.1'662—dc23
                            2014036554

ISBN: 978-1-60774-639-3
eBook ISBN: 978-1-60774-640-9

Printed in the United States of America

Author photo copyright © Lynn Parks

Design by Margaux Keres

10 9 8 7 6 5 4 3 2 1

First Edition

CONTENTS

A NOTE FROM ELIZABETH

It always feels scary to tell secrets, you know?

... especially when your secrets give you the advantage.

After all, each year my team and I are the secret weapons of students from all over the world who want to attend the very best colleges and universities in the United States. We make ACT scores soar to such a degree that we all feel a little bit guilty about it. In fact, we offer such an edge that most of our students won't even tell their classmates they're working with us.

The observations and insights in *Acing the ACT* are my private, personal notes on the ACT. These notes are my own secret weapons. They're not the basics; they're what set my team and me apart.

So here I am, a little nervous to let the cat out of the bag.

I realized decades ago that I'm someone who's naturally great at taking standardized tests; all I needed to do was figure out how to explain my approach and methods so anyone could use them and improve. I eventually became great at that, too; I've since spent well over a decade teaching students from New York to Athens, Beverly Hills to Miami, and Venezuela to Kuwait how to approach tests as I do.

All that teaching has given me a lot of time to observe.

I've observed what my students actually know—and what they really don't know. I've observed how they think and what they're afraid of.

I've observed how the test makers make the complex deceivingly simple and the simple deceivingly complex—what I call the "tricky" questions, the ones that students anguish over and often get wrong.

Most important, I've figured out how to get my students over those hurdles so they can create incredible score gains for themselves and get into their dream schools.

Even the trickiest questions on the ACT can be anticipated, as the test makers rely on similar question types year after year to stump students. We're focusing specifically on those types of questions in *Acing the ACT*. Again, this is all about secrets, tricks, weird questions, and a look at the meaner strategies of the ACT test makers.

Keep in mind that the ACT covers an enormous amount of material and there is simply no way we could include everything here, but don't worry! We've put together a package of free resources at http://AcingTheACTBook.com where you'll find not only all of the free, *real* ACT practice tests from the last ten years, but also a list of questions from those tests that correspond directly with the secrets in *Acing the ACT*. This book will be useful without these materials, but I'd strongly recommend you read this book with the guide to questions within reach to reinforce the strategies you'll learn here.

Good luck—and let's get started!

INTRODUCTION:
Know What You're Getting Into

THE PURPOSE OF EACH SUBSECTION OF THE ACT ISN'T CLEAR TO MOST TEST TAKERS.

The ACT includes four test sections: English, Mathematics, Reading, and Science, plus an optional Writing section (an essay that, incidentally, many colleges require). It could be argued that the purpose of every section is different than the purpose of the others—and this goes far beyond topic.

The English and the Math sections largely test *what* you know. You might even say that 75 percent of these sections are testing facts and skills: grammar rules, math formulas, rules of writing mechanics, translating English into algebra, and so on. The other 25 percent may be questions about *how* and *why* we use these rules.

Meanwhile, the Reading and Science sections are an inversion of that: They're all about application. They investigate *how* students think and process information, and include far fewer questions about information students might know ahead of time. In fact, it is incredibly rare for these sections to ask students to know a fact like a definition or a specific scientific term that would have been learned in school.

This means that the best way to see scores increase quickly is to focus on three things.

First, learn the facts and skills tested in the English and Math sections.

Second, understand strategy and how the Reading and Science sections apply reasoning in standardized ways.

Third (and this is what brings home those top scores), students should develop connoisseurship of ACT-style tricky questions. We have fit as many of these insights as we could into *Acing the ACT* and have developed codes for their styles so you can understand them even more easily; you'll find out more in the section about note-taking below.

STUDENTS ARE SUPERSTITIOUS AND FOLLOW THE PATTERN OF ANSWERS, THEREBY PSYCHING THEMSELVES OUT AND SOMETIMES EVEN CHANGING THEIR (CORRECT) ANSWERS.

The pattern of answer choices on the ACT is computer generated. Honestly, it's completely randomized, and yet so often students say, "Oh, I saw too many Es in a row, and that freaked me out, so I changed my answer to C."

Paying attention to the pattern in the answer choices is the death knell for your confidence and sanity, but *changing* your answer because of the pattern on the answer sheet is off-the-charts nuts. I don't want to waste time on this but I'm deadly serious.

You know you've thought about whether the answer choice pattern matters. The pattern doesn't matter. Period.

NOBODY KNOWS HOW TO TAKE USEFUL, STRATEGIC NOTES.

The scope of the ACT is very broad, particularly the English and Math sections. It tests dozens upon dozens of topics. Not realizing this, students often don't take notes about their patterns, habits, and mistakes while they're studying; they use the "Oh, I'll just remember that" plan, particularly for little details. Let's face it: fifty tedious questions later, you won't remember what you had trouble with earlier.

Let's discuss how to take notes that will *actually help you score higher*.

First, you absolutely have to take notes on any practice tests you take. Don't rely on your memory. Get a notebook and a pencil (no, not a pen) and plan to take notes from the very beginning of your studies. The earlier in the process you do this, the easier it'll be to sort through stuff and start to recognize patterns in the types of errors you make; you need time to see the particular questions that make you stumble.

The path to your top score is buried under your personal patterns and habits.

Now, you want to go into your ACT prep knowing that there's actually a finite number of skills on which they're going to test you and a handful of different ways they test that material. It's up to you to track your experience.

Instead of approaching each practice question as a stand-alone problem, remember that you'll never see *exactly* the same problem ever again; you'll see only similar problems that address the same *skills* or that use the same question *styles* to test your knowledge of particular topics. That means that your notes need to do two very important things.

Your notes need to help you

> see the mistake you made on that particular question.

> remember the correct approach to that particular question style when you encounter it later.

If they don't do those two things, your notes will do little to help you remember and apply that concept or note on test day, when it really matters.

Let me give you an example of a useless note. They can look pretty legit, so you have to know what we're looking for. Recently, I had a student who wrote in his notebook about one particular problem the words *don't use decimals*.

His note to himself literally looked just like that in his notebook:

> *12. Don't use decimals.*

That was it!

It's true that on that particular question it was better to use fractions than decimals, but that isn't always the case, so "don't use decimals" wasn't good general advice. Not only did he not explain to himself why fractions were better on this individual problem, but he also had not written anything to help him on any question he'd see again.

A better note, the kind of note I teach top scorers to take, would say something like this:

> *12. Look for fraction problems that could involve canceling, especially when π is involved. Don't switch to decimals. Keep fractions and cancel when possible on an estimation problem.*

My students use an effective and easy categorization method for note-taking. It's useful for all note-taking at the high school and college level, but it's especially good for ACT prep. It's based on the understanding that whenever you incorrectly answer an ACT question, there are only three possible reasons that happened.

Let's take a look.

 ## MEMORIZATION: YOU NEED TO LEARN SOMETHING NEW OR REFRESH AN OLD SKILL.

The memorization category will be the first category of notes you take, and you're going to mark them in your notes with a code so that it stands out to you. In *Acing the ACT* I'll note these things with the symbol M. Put the same symbol in your own notes for anything you need to memorize.

You'll probably get some questions wrong because you legitimately didn't know the fact or skill being tested. Maybe you were missing a comma rule or you forgot your special triangles in geometry. Some questions on the ACT refer to things you probably haven't seen in years. Most kids never have a grammar course in school, so you may have never even learned the rules in the first place.

You'll want to write down every single thing you uncover that you need to understand and/or have memorized: formulas, methods, and rules. Believe me when I tell you this test has some serious scope, so start writing down everything that needs memorization ASAP.

Write it *all* down. Highlight it *all* with your ⓜ code. *Actually create a plan* to memorize all of it.

Memorizing and reviewing what you've memorized should take up 10 to 15 minutes of your day, max, if you start prepping early enough.

Waiting until the last minute not only makes the memorization more difficult, but also gives you fewer opportunities to apply those formulas in real-time practice. Don't slack!

Ⓣ TRICKY QUESTIONS: THE SPECIAL ACT SETUP OR QUESTION PHRASING CONFUSED YOU.

These are the ones with the bad rap, the "trick" questions, the ones that make students mad, confusing them and burning up their precious time.

I'm not down with the "trick" question ethos; I like to call these guys the *tricky* questions because they're just creative, not necessarily super difficult or super mean. The ACT is very predictable in the ways it makes easy tasks challenging. Since this is the book of secrets, most of what we cover in *Acing the ACT* addresses tricky questions.

Notes about tricky questions are meant to illustrate how you got something wrong even though you knew all of the technical rules needed for the question. You were somehow confused or misled by the way the ACT question was asked; the way the game is played got the best of you. For all of the memorization you need to do, it's even more important to write things down like

 Q 27. I knew I needed the radius but I didn't see that I had to use the circumference formula to find it.

So much of *Acing the ACT* is dedicated to these particular questions because they embody what makes the ACT the ACT. You'll want to look at these tricky questions even if you're coming into this test with a solid score.

E: Human Error: You make mistakes just like everyone else.

The biggest mistake students make is not tracking their "careless errors." Personally, I don't believe these errors are actually careless; they're habitual—and it's possible to stop making them if you keep track of them.

Some parts of human error you can't control, and that's fine; that's the main reason I never let my students set perfection as their goal on the ACT. Perfection is a worthless pursuit, and not even a perfect score will guarantee your acceptance at top schools.

That said, some people make the same mistakes over and over. Errors that qualify as "careless" might include constantly overlooking negative signs on the Math section or misreading the same sorts of graphs on the Science section. A surprisingly reliable way to stop making these types of mistakes is to notice and log when you make them.

Seriously, if you make a mistake like not answering the question or incorrectly copying the problem, write down the exact mistake you made every time it happens and put a big (É) next to it. Believe me, once you see that you constantly screw up, say, semicolon questions, you're going to start caring, noticing, and not making that mistake anymore.

Remember, there are only three kinds of mistakes: (M), (T), and (É). Everything you'll see will fall into one of those categories; take advantage of that organization system early on. Logging every kind of error you make gives you a nuanced understanding of your personal experience with the test, of why your score might be below your goal, and of what you personally need to do to fix that.

Let's dig into each test.

THE ENGLISH
TEST

Overview: The English section includes 75 questions about punctuation, mechanics, and seemingly subjective editing topics answered in 45 minutes. These questions are spread over the course of 5 short passages, and questions are asked in context. Speed and accuracy are critical. Roughly 9 questions wrong drops a perfect score of 36 to a 29 (the 91st percentile); 15 to 18 questions wrong drops a score to a 25 (the 78th percentile). While it may not sound too difficult to stay above these thresholds, highly strategic sabotage is built in to the test by way of extremely tricky questions that makes hanging on to those points challenging if you don't know what to look for. It gets wild, but here are simple, strategic ways to improve your score.

You NEED TO READ THE ENTIRE PASSAGE FOR REASONS YOU TRULY AREN'T EXPECTING.

The test makers know you probably aren't reading the entire passage, and they sabotage you in ways you haven't considered. The reading passages and the corresponding question placement are pointedly designed to make you think that you can get away with not reading the passages as you go along. It's easy to become convinced that you don't need to read the passages when, truthfully, it's easy to answer a majority of the questions without having read the entire passage. *That's how they get you.*

Moreover, the best-hidden questions of this type are usually already perfect, correct stand-alone sentences. Most students would never think twice when they see them. "Oh, that's easy," they think—and they lose a point. One way the test makers trick you is by switching tense in such a way that you might not even notice.

Can they really hide something as simple as the wrong tense from even the best students?

Oh yes.

A classic way the ACT does this is by switching up past and present tense once it has got you in the groove of answering in a different tense.

Take the following example:

> America's schoolchildren were the beneficiaries of Jake Schmidt's vision, dynamic, and artistic expertise.
>
> F. NO CHANGE
> G. had been
> H. would have been
> J. are

That sounds fine, right?

Of course it does. What we're seeing here is an issue of context: if you just read the isolated sentence and if you haven't been reading the entire passage as you go along, you're very likely to select NO CHANGE.

After all, that sentence is grammatically correct.

What you're not seeing, though, is that our sentence is not contextually correct.

What's more, even if you had been reading the whole passage, it's *still* easy to make this mistake. Why? In this passage, we would have read about the founding and growth of a non-profit art movement that began thirty years ago. Most of the passage is in past tense, because it tells the story of how the organization came into existence. It was incorporated. It grew to a midsize company. It flourished.

In fact, most of the answer choices we would have selected throughout the passage would put answers into past tense, so we'd be in that habit by the time we get to a question like this—which, incidentally, is often dropped on us as maybe the fourteenth or fifteenth question in a passage. We're not thinking present tense, and the test makers know it.

Here's the trick: The organization that we've been reading about doesn't close its doors in the passage. It's still open for business, which means that America's school children *are* the beneficiaries of the company's founder's vision and expertise.

The action of the story happened in the past, so we talk about it in past tense, but the business and story continue on, so we move into present. Therefore, the answer is J.

Again, anyone who doesn't read the entire passage categorically gets this wrong.

ALWAYS READ EVERY WORD OF A SENTENCE YOU'RE GOING TO CHANGE BEFORE CHOOSING YOUR ANSWER.

The test makers know that when you're going for speed, you usually aren't even reading the whole sentence before you choose an answer. You might not catch yourself doing it, and that's by design, too. Where the underlined portion of the question stops and starts is manipulated—*totally* engineered—and the test makers do so strategically on a sentence-by-sentence basis. They do this so students who aren't reading the whole passage will miss passage-related questions *plus* those questions specifically designed to be misleading if the student stops reading midsentence and jumps to the answer choices.

I get into arguments about this all the time. I tell students they have to read the whole thing, like some overbearing crazy person, and they "yeah yeah yeah" me. Then we get to this kind of question, usually the second or third we see when we begin lessons, and they get it wrong because they weren't reading the whole sentence.

It's as if they think I like to hear the sound of my own voice while I dole out advice!

So, I've said it a million times in sessions, and I'll say it to you, too: You have to read the entire sentence before you begin to answer the question. Period.

An easy way to trap a student is to create a sentence with an underlined portion at its beginning that reads perfectly through that underlined portion but changes structure after the portion in question. For example, we might see a question in a sentence that reads,

> *Originally, the quarterback's family <u>that was gathered in the end zone</u>, celebrating his record-setting game.*

If a student stops reading after *end zone*, which many students do, the sentence sounds fine. They pick NO CHANGE and don't bother to read to the end of the sentence.

If we read to the end of the sentence, however, we'll see that the subject and verb are missing from the sentence; the quarterback's family isn't doing anything. The word *that* demotes *was gathered in the end zone* into descriptive material. To correct this sentence, we have to ditch *that*:

> *Originally, the quarterback's family was gathered in the end zone, celebrating his record-setting game.*

You wouldn't know it unless you'd read up to the end of the sentence. It's a costly point to lose, and this question style appears on most tests.

You'll need to learn to recognize overly verbose or redundant writing on the test, which is tough for a teenage ear.

High school writers unknowingly develop a super wordy style because their high school assignments are based on length, so it stands to reason that they often have trouble identifying verbosity on the ACT. You guys know how to find the longest possible ways to say things; after all, word count above all!

To the high school ear, *verbose* sounds *fancy*. For example, if you find on the ACT phrases like *due to the fact that* or *owing to the fact that*, what the writer really means is *because*.

The rule of thumb is this: The ACT always wants the shortest way to say something, provided it's (a) grammatically correct and (b) doesn't include slang.

The fewer words the better.

The other thing to pay attention to is redundancy. *Redundancy* means the appearance of repetitive language in a sentence—literally, saying the same thing twice. This can mean using exactly the same word multiple times or multiple phrases with the same meaning or intention.

Redundancies come in two main types.

1. REDUNDANCY INSIDE THE UNDERLINED PORTION OF THE SENTENCE

The most simple versions of these include the redundant material right in the underlined portion.

> The various kinds of each ornament can be displayed separately.
>
> F. NO CHANGE
>
> G. Each
>
> H. Each unique individual
>
> J. Each single, unique

You should be able to hear that too much is going on here: we can say *the various ornaments can be displayed* or *each ornament can be displayed*. Saying both is too much, so in this case you should replace the phrase with *Each* and be done with it. You'll see several of these on every test and, almost always, the answer is just the single-word answer.

2. REDUNDANCY OUTSIDE THE UNDERLINED PORTION OF THE SENTENCE

The ACT sets precedents of expected answer styles throughout the test. We've already seen it with tense questions. It happens in redundancy questions, too.

When a student is moving quickly—and when she's already seen examples of verbose, redundant answer choices that were all enclosed in the underlined portion like the one we saw above—she's less likely to consider that the sentence may be redundant in places that aren't underlined. The test sets you up to expect that all redundancy will be underlined for you, and then it hides the redundancy elsewhere in a question later in the test:

> <u>Originally, the muffin company</u> was a full bakery and café that also offered coffee and small home goods at its inception.
>
> A. NO CHANGE
>
> B. At first, it
>
> C. It, starting out,
>
> D. The muffin company

Again, it's easier to get drawn into an incorrect answer if you aren't reading the entire sentence before answering the question. If you stop at the word *coffee*, which many do, you'll get this wrong because you won't reach the phrase *at its inception*, which we have to keep in the sentence because it isn't underlined. To clarify, the meaning *when the shop opened* is captured in *at its inception*, so it's redundant to include the word *Originally* as well.

A lot of the time students feel so confident (and are so fixated on speed) that they won't even read all the answer choices when the sentence seems correct as is. The test makers intentionally make the option without the redundant content, D, the last choice. Only the last answer choice hints that the question may be one with redundant content.

YOU'LL NEED TO UNDERSTAND HOW VOCABULARY IS TESTED ON THE ACT; THE RUMORS THAT IT ISN'T AREN'T TRUE.

One of the driving reasons that students preferred the ACT to the SAT (before the SAT was redesigned) is that the ACT does not have any sort of sentence completion section that directly tests high-level vocabulary. Given that the overwhelming majority of students, even those at top schools, are missing that advanced vocabulary, it makes sense they'd avoid it. You'll hear people say there isn't any vocabulary on the ACT, but that's inaccurate.

What the ACT does is something actually more covert than the SAT: It tests students' knowledge of the nuanced differences between closely related, albeit mid-level, words. The tested words are far more common, but the questions require significant consideration . . . and that's really the point. The ACT people want to know you know why you're using the language you're using, and if you're being pointed and purposeful in your sentence structure and word choice.

Here's how they check that:

1. REAL REDUNDANCY

Sometimes vocabulary questions test whether you recognize the most straightforward example of redundancy: listed words that are truly synonymous. The idea here is to use as few words as possible without losing meaning.

A typical question will read like this:

> *Marvin entered the room* <u>holding, clasping, and grasping</u> *the camera bag.*

Answer choices will include various combinations of the three underlined words, and the final option will narrow the portion down to one verb, *holding*. Unless the three underlined words are *very* different in individual meaning, your best bet is always to go with the most succinct way to express the idea in the sentence and to choose the single-word answer choice.

2. REAL DIFFERENCES IN MEANING

Rather than listing redundant words, thereby insinuating that they're synonymous, real meaning questions ask students to choose between words purely based on their meaning, just like a regular vocabulary question. The thing is, the words offered as options will mean *nearly* the same thing; sometimes they're easy for students to parse out, sometimes they're not so much.

Take the words *decide, know,* and *suppose*. These three words have related meanings, but they are not at all synonymous. *Decide* means to *pick* or *choose*, whereas *know* means to be aware of something. Meanwhile, *suppose* means to assume or guess—or maybe even acquiesce.

Similarly, another question has us choose between *compress*, *contract*, and *reduce*. In this case it's all about who is doing the action: If something is being *compressed*, a force is pressing down on it to make it smaller. If something is *contracting*, it's shrinking on its own, independent of an outside force (but maybe because something has been applied to it). To *reduce*, though, is to lessen something, to minimize it.

While you won't see major vocabulary on the ACT, you *will* see this sort of choosing between related words, and it's important to slow down and define each word carefully for yourself before selecting the most appropriate word.

3. APPROPRIATE ADVERBS AND TRANSITIONS

I want to address the importance of understanding the meaning of adverbs and general transition phrases for the ACT. These are words you would not normally think about.

Usually writing like a teenager is not synonymous with being pithy, specific, and mechanically exact. Naturally, then, the ACT tests the best, most efficient, and most appropriate words for creating solid writing structure and clarity—something most students don't practice.

Students have to know the true meanings of all of the following:

› *however, by contrast, on the contrary, conversely, meanwhile, although, nevertheless*

› *therefore, thus*

› *for example, to illustrate, in fact*

› *on the one hand*

› *on the other hand*

› *additionally, moreover*

› *in that, since, as*

› *second, finally*

› *in addition, in summary, in contrast*

I've grouped these words by similar meaning, but you are also expected to understand what they mean individually. I often have students create this list of words as they come across them in their practice tests, and I have them actually define them (yes, using the dictionary) so they're absolutely sure they know what they mean. These words are most often used to specifically highlight the relationship between two ideas or sentences. When you're linking two sentences in an English section question, you'll need to read the *entire* previous sentence and the *entire* follow-up sentence all the way to its end *before* you choose the appropriate word.

You'll never be asked to choose between using almost totally synonymous words in this instance; that would be unfair. Thus, if you see *thus* and *therefore* used exactly the same way (don't forget to make sure that the answer choices use equivalent punctuation), you won't be choosing between them purely based on meaning. That also means, strategically, that neither of them could be correct.

Special note: For whatever reason, *on the other hand* appears with some frequency on the ACT in this manner. I have no idea why it's so important, but the ACT people often stump students because it will be shown on its own, rather than with its counterpart *on one hand*. Here's the rule: you don't need to have used the phrase *on one hand* in order to appropriately use the phrase *on the other hand*.

THE **ACT** IS NOT A SPELLING TEST, BUT SPELLING MATTERS IN WAYS YOUR SMARTPHONE MAKES MORE DIFFICULT.

Thanks to homophones, lazy American English pronunciation, horrible texting habits, and the totally unreliable smartphone autocorrect features, many teenagers hear—and write— entirely incorrect grammar and spelling.

One of the best bets for success on the English and Reading sections is to read daily. I recommend students read articles in *Vanity Fair*, *Wired*, *The New Yorker*, or *The Economist*, as these often include articles of appropriate reading level that are written in a similar structure to ACT passages. While daily reading is especially important for those students who do not speak or read English on a daily basis, most American students do not read periodicals and spend most of their free media time watching video and reading poorly composed and autocorrected text messages. More than ever, reading matters, and modern students are struggling because they're reading less than ever.

Here's where this issue most commonly rears its ugly head:

1. SHOULD'VE, WOULD'VE, COULD'VE

I promise you that as I sit and write this, I just received a text message that read, "I would of done anything to meet Bob

Ross." Maybe you make this mistake differently; maybe you say, "We should of gotten pizza instead of McDonald's."

Maybe you don't immediately see the problem here; that's common. This is a classic mistake, though—and it appears on the ACT for that reason.

American-spoken conversation continually uses contractions, and one of those contractions is constantly mispronounced: when we mean to say *have* (or more often the contraction *'ve*), we usually pronounce it *of*. The ACT test makers know this and will often offer *of* as an alternative answer choice to *'ve* and *have*, and using *of* is 100 percent incorrect.

The text I received should have said, *I would've done anything to meet Bob Ross.*

The big four instances you want to look out for on the ACT (and in life!) are *should've*, *would've*, *could've*, and *might've*. They're totally interchangeable with *should have*, *would have*, *could have*, and *might have*. Never *of*. You won't be asked to choose between *'ve* or *have* in the answer choices.

2. YOU HAD BETTER

Another way students' ears are tested is in the very rarely written-down long form of the phrase *you'd better*. We're always saying aloud, "You'd better hurry up!" Very few students know that when we say *you'd better*, we're really saying *you had better hurry up*, and the ACT knows this. Expect to see answer choices that include the unfamiliar long form alongside other wildly incorrect options.

ANY FORM OF THE VERB *TO BE* SHOULD BE SEEN AS A RED FLAG.

The ACT uses *to be*—the most common verb in the English language and the one we almost always use correctly in conversation—in the most unexpected ways. The test makers use its familiarity against us and test it in all its forms.

RED FLAG VERBS

am	*was*	*being*	*has*
is	*were*	*been*	*have*
are	*be*		*had*

Anytime you see any form of the verb *to be* in an answer choice, you want to see major red flags. You'll also want to keep an eye out for the auxiliary verbs *has*, *have*, and *had*. You don't need to know what they're called, but you need to know they matter.

First, you have to understand that the reason this is so tricky is actually *because* you use your knowledge of subject-verb agreement all day, every day. Just like in the homophone spelling questions from earlier, your ear is being tested and used against you.

You know that we say that dogs *run* but a dog *runs*. It's the sort of thing you're very unlikely to screw up in regular conversation because your ear runs the show and usually does so pretty well. That's exactly why it's tested here; it's easy for the test makers to engineer a "gotcha!" moment on the ACT and knock you down a point.

It sounds a bit like I'm accusing the ACT test makers of being a little bit against you. I suppose in this case they are.

1. *BEING* AND WHETHER OR NOT THE UNDERLINED PORTION REQUIRES A VERB

We'll kill two birds with one stone here. Take a look at the following example:

> *This year one of my summer camp's exchange* <u>*students being*</u> *Natalia Jotevic, who came* from Russia.
>
> F. NO CHANGE
>
> G. students was
>
> H. students,
>
> J. students, named

First, you must be aware of the most tricky form of the verb *to be*, the word *being*. High school writers tend to overuse it—usually improperly—so whenever it pops up, you need to take notice.

The only times we can use the word *being* is in a case like *the cats were being quiet* or in the idiomatic phrase *that being said*. Otherwise, the vast majority of the time, *being* is used incorrectly on the ACT. Be aware that if you're choosing *being* on the ACT, you had better be extremely confident that every other answer choice is dead wrong.

Clearly, this is all to say that we should be suspect of the given sentence above.

Next, let's look at everything else that's built into our example sentence. It should be part of your strategy to recognize that *some* of these answer choices include verbs but *one does not*. If some of the answer choices have verbs and others don't, all sorts of sirens in your head should start screamimg, "DECIDE WHETHER YOU NEED A VERB!"

This is another case in which if you do not read this entire sentence, if you read only up to the girl's name—as so many students do—you will likely choose answer choice H and get the question wrong.

Now, it's also important that you understand that the subject of this sentence is the word *one*. The rest of that stuff, *of my summer camp's exchange student*, is a prepositional phrase. It's there to distract you from that singular subject *one*. Here's a list of prepositions that you should keep an eye out for.

about	beside(s)	following	off
across	between	for	on
after	beyond	from	onto
among	concerning	in	opposite
around	considering	inside	outside
as	despite	into	over
at	down	like	past
before	during	minus	plus
behind	except(ing)	near	regarding
beneath	excluding	of	round

save	to	up	with
since	toward(s)	upon	within
than	under	versus	without
through	until	via	

It's in your best interest to draw a line through prepositional phrases in sentences so you can more easily see the relationship between the subject and the verb, and identify what needs to agree with what. You're looking to find the short, structural frame of the sentence: subject, verb, object.

The short version of the sentence above, one that just includes the basics, reads,

> ~~This year~~ one of my summer camp's exchange students being Natalia Jotevic, who came from Russia.

When you break it down like this, to find the subject, verb, and object, it's easier to see the sentence *definitely needs a new verb*. That verb must match "one" so you'll choose G.

2. EAR-CONFUSING SINGULAR-PLURAL SUBJECT-VERB AGREEMENT

But wait! It gets worse.

Just like in the last example, in which we had the subject *one*, the most advanced versions of these questions are designed to go beyond tense or verb-or-no-verb and, instead, pointedly mess with your ear. Essentially, these sentences will choose a singular subject and throw in a litany of plural words in prepositional phrases right after it, so when it comes time to pick a verb (usually paired with a form of *to be*), you've totally forgotten you're dealing with a singular subject and will pop in a plural verb . . . and get it wrong.

The thing is, it just sounds weird to most people to use a singular verb after a plural noun, and that's where the ACT people get you.

> Not one of the many people in clown costumes
> were wearing the appropriate safety gear.
>
> A. NO CHANGE
>
> B. was wearing
>
> C. were actually wearing
>
> D. have been wearing

Here, we've heard the word *people*. We've heard the word *costumes*. Yet, we have to go with the answer that includes *was* because we have to match the case of the subject of the sentence, *one*, not merely the last word we heard, which is what our ear wants us to do. Again, the easiest way to identify the subject in the sentence, the word *one*, is to cross out the prepositional phrases *of the many people* and *in clown costumes*; again, you should actually cross right through those words in your test booklet.

You won't just see the pronoun *one*, though, in instances of misleading singular subjects. You'll see all sorts of singular verbs that you think are plural: words like *business, company, country, board, school, committee,* and *group*. Naturally, the test makers will throw in a plural verb with singular words in prepositional phrases, too, so you absolutely must pay attention.

It seems simple enough, but there are more than one of these on each test, and if you miss them, you lose really valuable points.

3. PAGE PLACEMENT MATTERS: WHERE THE TEST MAKERS PLAY DIRTY

They'll make these questions that much worse by making sure that the subject is on the previous page. They're counting on "out of sight, out of mind" happening to you. For example, maybe *Not one of* will be on the bottom of the previous page, and the verbs with which it agrees are at the top of the next page, so you're even less inclined to go back and identify the case than you would have been anyway. Then they'll fill the sentence with multiple prepositional phrases to totally hijack your ear by the time you get to the verb.

You might see a sentence like

> *Not one of the loud trucks*
>
> *and buses filled with people and their belongings would be parked in their correct spot.*

By the time you read the words *trucks*, *buses*, *people*, and *belongings*, you (and your ear) have completely forgotten about that long-lost singular verb on the previous page.

This is classic ACT meanness. It feels vindictive. Always read from the beginning of a sentence, especially if it appears on the previous page.

4. PARALLELISM WITH MULTIPLE VERBS (OR DISTRIBUTIVE SUBJECT-VERB AGREEMENT)

Let's switch into math mode for a moment. We should know from algebra the basics of distribution: If we see an expression like $x(p + n)$, we should know that the x distributes to (or pairs with) the p and n. Our expression could be written as $xp + xn$.

This structure tells us that *x* relates to *p* and *n*, even though it doesn't appear right next to them when they're in parentheses.

The same thing happens in grammar, especially with subjects and multiple verbs: subjects "distribute" to verbs. It's a little trickier, though, in grammar because we don't have the luxury of parenthesis and +/- signs to show us what's related to what. The correct distribution is called "parallelism," and that's what the test makers want to see if you know.

Take this example sentence:

> *Gabriel wanted to wash the car with soap and*
> *dry it as quickly as possible.*

Here we see that Gabriel wants to do two things: *wash* the car and *dry* it. I kept the words *wash* and *dry* in the same form so that they would both match up with the *to* that comes earlier in the sentence.

Often I'll write an example sentence like this so students can really see the structure:

> *Gabriel wanted to*
> 1. <u>wash</u> the car with soap
> and
> 2. <u>dry</u> it as quickly as possible.

When we write the sentence like this, it's a little easier to see that *to* matches up with *wash* and *dry*, and so we need to make sure, then, that *wash* and *dry* match up with *to*. Parallelism is a matter of writer's preference in some ways, so don't get wedded to one idea of it.

It's also entirely acceptable to slightly change this sentence and distribute the *to* with the verbs, also:

Gabriel wanted to wash the car with soap and to dry it as quickly as possible.

Gabriel wanted

1. to wash the car with soap

and

2. to dry it as quickly as possible.

In this case, *wanted* is distributing to *to wash* and *to dry*.

Naturally, the ACT authors are inclined to make things tricky: they want that *x* subject to be as far away as it can possibly be from its multiple verbs. They may even, again, spread the sentence over two different pages.

I know I could walk in that studio anytime, and someone

would look up from painting a landscape or glazing a bowl and wink and smiles at me.

A. NO CHANGE

B. winking and smiling

C. winked and smile

D. wink and smile

Break these sentences down to the bare minimum subjects and verbs so you can see what needs to match:

. . . someone would

1. look up

from painting a landscape or glazing a bowl

and

2. wink and smile

at me.

You can even go so far as to think that *someone . . . would . . . smile at me*. That *would* is literally fourteen words away, but it still dictates the form of that verb *smile*.

REVIEW THE SINGULAR AND PLURAL POSSESSIVES, ESPECIALLY IF YOU'RE A BIG FAN OF TEXT MESSAGING.

Singular and plural possessives are perfect for misleading and outright tricking students because most students haven't had a real grammar course—and because such issues are often inaccurately autocorrected on smartphones.

1. GENERAL RULES FOR PLURAL POSSESSIVE

First, we need to know how to use apostrophes to show possession in regular words. It's best to just memorize the rule:

> *dogs*: plural (We took our [multiple] dogs to the park.)
>
> *dog's*: singular possessive (The [one] dog's bed is round.)
>
> *dogs'*: plural possessive (The [many] dogs' leashes were on the floor).

The ACT often compounds plural possessives, and it happens multiple times on each test. You really have to break these down in order to execute them correctly.

A compound plural possessive (which, again, appears on every test at least once) would involve two possessive words piggybacked on each other, and students need to specify the appropriate form of both words. Look at this example:

> *After three hours of having been worn while the girls played in the snow, the <u>girls jackets</u> sleeves were completely soaked through.*

Here we have to identify whether two words should be plural or plural possessive: *girls* and *jackets*. In this case, it's the *jackets* that belong to the *girls*, so we need *girls'*, and then the sleeves that belong to the *jackets*, so we need *jackets'* as well, as in choice D.

> A. girls jackets'
>
> B. Jess and Erin's jackets
>
> C. girl's jackets
>
> D. girls' jackets'

You'll always be offered all sorts of combinations of singular, plural, and plural possessive, and it's always best to break them down individually for analysis. A great rule of thumb is to remember that whenever you can effectively substitute the words *his*, *her*, or *its* for the word you're considering making possessive, you use the apostrophe. Otherwise, you're dealing with an apostrophe-free plural. Likewise, if you can legitimately substitute the word *their* for the word you're considering making plural and it makes sense, you will use the plural possessive form of the word, which is often the form with the apostrophe at the end of the word (like *jackets'*).

2. *ITS*, *IT'S*, AND (*ITS'*?)

Next, let's review the difference between *its*, *it's*, and *its'*. The easiest way to remember the difference between *its* and *it's* is to think of the apostrophe in *it's* as the dot of the missing *i* in the contraction of *it is*. Basically, you know *it's* is correct when you can swap in the words *it is* in the sentence and it makes sense. Meanwhile, *its* shows possession (as in *The cat licks its paws*). This makes kids crazy because we usually pair an apostrophe with a possessive, but with *its* we don't.

Moreover, your smartphone (at least as of this writing) does not grammatically autocorrect. If you type *its*—even if you're using it correctly—most phones will change it back to *it's*. Be aware.

You'll notice that I added the word *its'* up in the header. Let this serve as a super tricky warning: often the ACT will offer the word *its'* as an answer choice, which is particularly evil because *its'* is *not a real word*. There are only two words you need to know, *its* and *it's*.

3. *WHO'S* AND *WHOSE*

Who's versus *whose* is another ear issue, and the ACT people are counting on you to mix them up. Just like *it's* is really *it is*, *who's* is *who is*. Again, that apostrophe is like the dot in the *i* in *is*. Meanwhile, *whose* is possessive.

Here are the two words in action:

Who's *going to the Phillies game?* Who is *going to the Phillies game?*

Whose *hat are you wearing to the Phillies game?* possessive

4. WORDS THAT ARE PLURAL BY DEFINITION

Another element of confusion enters when we have words that are already plural without an s, like the word *women*. In these cases we'd say *The* women's *league is running an auction*, not *the womens's league*. Similar words include *men*, *teeth*, *children*, *people*, *phenomena*, and *fish*. Be sure to consider the meaning of words when you apply punctuation.

EVEN THOUGH IT'S WRITING, GRAMMATICAL EDITING ON THE ACT IS NOT A MATTER OF OPINION.

Go into the ACT understanding that every question has a factually correct answer. While the English content editing questions may *feel* subjective, every question's response must be factually *objective*.

The ACT asks you to do a lot of content editing—adding and deleting sentences, moving paragraphs, and deciding whether or not to include particular details. It's difficult for a student who is empowered to write independently and edit his own writing—and even the writing of his friends—to let go of the subjective, opinion-based editing that happens in the context of writing at school.

Moreover, when students read in school and for personal pleasure, they read for general ideas, looking for the gist of what the author is saying, and the ACT does *not* reward that. That matters in Reading, of course, but it also bites students on the English section.

The ACT rewards technical specificity at all times.

That's what makes these questions particularly challenging. They *feel* as though they inquire about writing *preference*, so when the correct answer may not be at all to the student's taste, he'll avoid it. The most important things a student can do are:

> (a) be totally clear on what the question is asking

> and

> (b) always focus on why an answer choice is the best objective choice according to the ACT.

Again, it's important when faced with these editing questions on the ACT to switch the mind-set from preference to provability. Every word written on the ACT—both in the questions and in the answer choices—matters and has been specifically, strategically chosen. Gist is irrelevant; meaning is everything.

1. CHOOSING APPROPRIATE TRANSITION SENTENCES

A transition sentence, by definition, leads a reader from the last paragraph into the next paragraph. This means that it's not possible to choose an appropriate transition between two paragraphs *without having read both of them*. Many students hesitate to read beyond a question because it feels odd and wasteful to read through several more questions to get to the end of the paragraph. So they don't do it, but then they have no real idea what the next paragraph is about.

I usually describe the relationship between two adjacent paragraphs using colors: When you're choosing a transition sentence to stick between a "red" paragraph and a "blue" paragraph, you want to be sure you have a little "red" and a little "blue" in that sentence. By that I mean that there is direct, repeated evidence from each paragraph in the transition, oftentimes the exact same words. Think matchy-matchy.

Remember that on the ACT we're looking for technique, not taste, so these transitions have to be mechanical.

> Learning to make pottery on the wheel—
> also known as "throwing pots"—is a popular
> pastime at our local art armory. Students in these
> community classes range in age from as young
> as in high school to well into retirement. The

student work is just as varied: students produce everything from bowls and mugs to teapots and vases.

It took me a long time to learn to make a teapot. Learning to use the wheel can test one's patience during the early stages. So many factors can contribute to a vessel that doesn't turn out as one intended: the way the clay is wedged, whether it's properly centered on the wheel to begin with, and how much moisture is in the clay can affect the result. Moreover, the potter's skill and technique play just as much a part in guiding the clay into a form that is consistent and holds up to firing.

Given that all of the following are true, which sentence provides the most appropriate transition from the first paragraph to the second?

A) You have to be careful when you're wedging, or kneading, clay.

B) At first, one might think that the term "throwing" comes from what a new potter feels like doing with the clay when it doesn't do what she intends.

C) Pottery isn't a hobby for people who aren't patient.

D) The wheel isn't the only thing tricky about making bowls and cups.

Remember, if one paragraph is "red" and the other paragraph is "blue", we want a little bit of "red" and a little bit of "blue" in our transition sentence. We see that in choice B: we see the word *throwing* from the first paragraph and then we see the word *intends* from the second paragraph, as well as a full explanation of things that may prevent the potter from creating what she wants.

Be as literal as possible on these transitions—matchy-matchy is what works!

2. CHOOSING APPROPRIATE CONCLUSIONS

Again, we need to follow directions exactly as they're stated in the question. When we're instructed to choose a specific concluding sentence, we're almost always asked to keep that conclusion "relevant to the topic" or to the introduction of the passage.

Again, we like matchy-matchy, sometimes even the exact same words and phrases that we have already seen in the passage. Just as we look for "red" and "blue" in our transition sentences, we want that "red" in the conclusion if we had "red" in the introduction.

Think this way: imagine we see a passage that begins *Scientist Jane Goodall is a pioneer in researching primate relationships and behavior.* It would be perfectly reasonable on the ACT to say that the most appropriate conclusion to the passage would be a sentence like *Truly, pioneers like Jane Goodall have changed the way we understand primate relationships.* Many students shy away from these answers. "It seems too easy," they say. Keep it literal! Don't expect the ACT to get creative. *Do* expect it to follow the rule that concluding sentences *conclude.* They don't introduce new ideas or end with a cliff-hanger or kicker.

3. SUPPORTING THE AUTHOR OBJECTIVE: ADDING DETAILS AND IDENTIFYING MAIN THEMES

Most of the questions on the ACT English portion relate to small, underlined sections of sentences that are replaced by a more grammatically appropriate answer choice. It's intuitive and easy to move through fairly quickly, because those are the types of questions we associate with real, formal grammar rules.

The more subjective the answer choices seem to be, though, the more students tend to waffle.

Sometimes, though, the ACT offers a selection of true, new, statements and asks students to select the one that pro-vides the most relevant information with regards to a specific *objective* the author might have. This may involve replacing an entire sentence or adding in a new sentence. These sentences will be relevant to the topic of the paragraph they're in, and they'll be good for the general sense of "flow" of a paragraph.

Most important, the question will ask the student to select something extremely specific, and it is imperative that you don't skim over the specific objective of the question.

The question will sound like this:

> *Given that all of the following statements are true, which one if added at this point in the paragraph illustrates the narrator's sense of entitlement to the necklace?*

Every time you see a question like this, pointedly latch on to the objective of the question. In this case, it's *illustrating* something specific, the *sense of entitlement*. Only one answer choice will remotely address a sense of entitlement, and it's your job to choose that answer *even if you don't particularly like the details or you think you could have written something better yourself*. The goal here is to *follow directions*.

Let's look at some possible answer choices:

> A. My mother had always treasured that necklace.
>
> B. I had always thought the necklace matched my taste and personality.
>
> C. It made sense, then, that she should have given the necklace to me.
>
> D. The necklace was inlaid with diamonds and a few small emeralds.

Many students would wrestle between B and C, but the most important idea, again, is that sense of entitlement, of belonging. Even though the idea that it matches her taste and personality seems relevant, we have to focus on believing that she should *own* it, and C is the only choice that does so.

You'll see many of these on every test, and focusing on key details is most important. Typical questions involve details that

› give evidence of the narrator's "familiarity" with a person or thing.

› "further describe" an event, an object, or a person.

› "offer specific recommendations" to the reader.

> add "new and specific details" to a story.

> "illustrate" a particular quality of the narrator or a character in the passage.

Many students are afraid of these questions because they usually add new details, and for whatever reason, students hesitate to do so.

Do *not* be afraid to change or add in new details to a passage.

Moreover, if the question asks you to select an answer that does *two* things, like *illustrates the narrator's interest in* something and *supports the idea the passage is meant to be instructive*, you have to make sure your answer choice does *both* things.

Again, it's entirely acceptable to add new, *relevant* details to the ACT.

4. MAIN THEME

Our "red" and "blue" tool for matching up words and appropriate answer choices can help when looking at themes and primary purpose questions, too.

Very often the last question or two on each passage in the English section will inquire about overarching themes or purposes within those passages. Students struggle with these, again, because they don't "like" the answer choices—the options aren't descriptions that they themselves would choose to describe the passage.

Again, our goal is to get to the same answer as the test maker, and there's a clear way to do so. There are a few approaches to keep in mind here. First, the titles of the passages are included in the test for a reason: the titles usually blatantly allude to the major theme of the essay. Perhaps that Jane Goodall passage we'd talked about earlier had been called Primates Talking: Jane Goodall's Research Changes the Field. The essay might give us a paragraph or two about the state of primate research before Ms. Goodall came on the scene, but then the remainder of the passage will focus entirely on her work and its results.

Then we'll see a question like this:

> *Suppose the writer's goal had been to write a brief essay focusing on the history and development of primate research. Would this essay successfully fulfill this goal?*
>
> A. Yes, because the essay explains that not much had been known about primate communication and then explains the transformative work of one of its most important scientists.
>
> B. Yes, because the essay mentions how primate research has impacted research on communication methods of other species.
>
> C. No, because the essay refers to human communication in addition to primate communication.
>
> D. No, because the essay focuses on only one researcher, Jane Goodall.

The overwhelming majority of students will choose D because they think that they should see a survey of all of the primate scientists' work in a passage that addresses the development of primate research. On the ACT, though, we would choose A because we need to answer the question *exactly*. The title can help us do so confidently: We see a reference to Ms. Goodall and to her having changed "the field." We saw some history, and then we saw her impact on it.

Your best bet is to quickly review the title and topics of each paragraph in the passage—usually by reading the topic sentence—and to choose an answer that reflects both. When in doubt, use the title to provide clarity.

5. WHEN TO ADD DETAILS

Again, we have to remember that everything on the ACT has to be inarguably correct or incorrect, so we don't want to strike details as irrelevant unless they are *really* irrelevant. Like, *out there*. Moreover, just as we are comfortable striking things that don't connect, we should not add in details that veer away from the logical progression of the paragraph in which they're being placed.

One example of a classic question that includes an irrelevant detail could be a passage about the Civil War. The passage is entirely about factual history, and then it mentions a film about the particular battle. While the mention of the film is seen as pertinent supporting evidence to the importance of the battle, the passage then includes an interjection that Denzel Washington starred as a particular character in the movie about the war. It then goes right back to historical narrative.

That Denzel was in the movie is *not* relevant to a history passage. It may be interesting, but it does not in any way support the historical argument made in the rest of the paragraph. *That* is the sort of thing you should always scratch.

Keep in mind that it's easiest to identify when things are truly irrelevant if the train of thought returns to the previous idea *after* the detail you'd be inserting.

WHENEVER A PRONOUN APPEARS IN AN ANSWER CHOICE, IT'S IMPERATIVE TO RECOGNIZE IT AND IDENTIFY ITS ANTECEDENT IMMEDIATELY FOR MULTIPLE REASONS.

Every pronoun has what is known as an *antecedent.* You don't need to know the term, but you do need to know what it is, and that's simple: the antecedent is the noun that a pronoun refers to.

Check it out:

> Rory put *her* dress on a hanger.

In this sentence, *Rory* is the antecedent and *her* is the pronoun (otherwise we'd have to say *Rory put Rory's dress on a hanger*).

1. ADDING AN ANTECEDENT

It's important to know that just as adding details on the ACT is acceptable, provided they're related to the passage, it's also sometimes necessary to add an antecedent to a sentence. Sometimes this is for clarity, and sometimes the antecedent actually isn't in there to begin with.

> Josh told Mark that *he* could only use *his* tool kit if *he* promised to put everything back where *he* found it.

Here we have an issue of disambiguation: Since pronouns always refer back to the last named noun, we assume that every time we see *he* or *his*, the pronoun has to be referring back to the name *Mark*. However, from the context of the sentences, we'd be able to see that's not the authors meaning; the tool kit actually belongs to *Josh*. In order to make clear who has ownership and who is giving the instructions, we actually need to write,

> Josh told Mark that he could use Josh's tool kit only if Mark promised to put everything back where he found it.

You'll also sometimes need to replace a pronoun entirely with a noun that you haven't read about yet. This terrifies students, but on the ACT it is acceptable and expected:

> Devon loves his new roadster, accelerating as he races past them on his way to work.

You may notice in this sentence that the word *them* has no antecedent, no noun to which it directly points. In fact, you should be thinking, "Who the heck are we talking about here?"

Even if you had not heard of anyone else in the passage so far, on the ACT it's expected that you will replace the word *them* with a real noun for clarity's sake:

> Devon loves his new roadster, accelerating as he races past other drivers on his way to work.

Just as we're not afraid to add relevant details to a passage, so we shouldn't be afraid to replace pronouns with specific nouns, even if they have not yet appeared in the passage as we've been reading it.

2. PRONOUNS: WHO AND WHOM

Who and *whom* are on the ACT often, and they're often used incorrectly in spoken American English, so most students have no idea what the real difference is between them.

I could tell you that *who* is a subject pronoun and *whom* is a direct object pronoun, but that usually doesn't do anyone a whole lot of good, either. The easiest way to remember what's what is to remember which words *who* and *whom* relate to. In short, we use *who* to replace subject pronouns *she*, *he*, and *I*. We use *whom* to replace *her*, *him*, and *me*. Some people like to remember this by associating the *m* at the end of *whom* with the *m* at the end of *him*.

We might say, *Who was on the phone?* . . . and the real, grammatical response is, *It was she*.

Likewise, we might say, *To whom did Leigh send the letter?* . . . and the official response is, *She sent it to him*.

There are never any really complex uses of *who* and *whom* that you'll have to haggle over; they're straightforward moments in which you're rewarded for knowing the difference between the two.

3. GO WITH THE PRECEDENT WHEN IT COMES TO *YOU*

It's standard for teachers of college prep English classes to discourage students from using the word *you* in their formal writing assignments, and for good reason: It's not appropriate for formal, argumentative writing. Because teachers are so heavy-handed about not using *you*, and rightly so, students are disinclined to think that it would be acceptable on the ACT . . . so, of course, it is.

If the ACT sets the precedent of using *you* throughout an instructive or informative passage and then asks us to choose between appropriate pronouns, it's fine (and recommended) to stick with *you*. Moreover, the ACT usually takes the stance that using *you* actually *is* more direct.

PAY ATTENTION TO THE WORD *THESE*. IT MEANS SO MUCH MORE THAN WE THINK. SERIOUSLY.

Just like auxiliary verbs alert students to challenging questions, we can rely on the article *these* to guide us on some of the more complex, seemingly subjective editing questions. We've already seen several instances in which we're asked to insert new sentences into an existing paragraph. There *always* has to be a specific reason why the correct sentence is officially appropriate, and *these* is often the evidence—even if it's several sentences away.

Take the following short paragraph, for example:

> *After months, or sometimes more than a year of active duty, soldiers come home. The stresses of returning to civilian life can be profound. These animals—usually dogs—are trained to perform all sorts of tasks, from helping around the house to providing security and companionship to their new owners.*
>
> Which choice is the most effective first sentence of Paragraph 3?
>
> F. NO CHANGE
>
> G. Some veterans benefit from a service animal when they return home from active duty.

H. Most people agree that being a soldier is a very admirable job.

J. Returning to active duty, soldiers can't wait to come home to their pets.

Even if we read through the second sentence of this paragraph, to the word *profound*, everything seems fine—and we might choose NO CHANGE if we don't read the paragraph in its entirety. If we continue to read through sentence three, though, things get a little weird. We suddenly see a reference to "These animals," which comes out of nowhere.

When we use the word *these*, sometimes we use it in a way that implies specificity or to say "these [whatever] about which we were already talking." In the paragraph as it stands now, there hasn't been any mention of animals—even though *these* is telling us they're specific animals we should already have heard about—which means we have to go back and put the animals in ourselves. In this case, G would be our best option.

Whenever you're asked to add a new sentence to the paragraph, always look for directly related details and keep an eye out for the word *these*, even if it's several sentences away.

THERE ARE RULES FOR SENTENCE STRUCTURE, PARTICULARLY ABOUT MODIFIERS, AND IT'S LIKELY THAT IF YOU'RE AN AMERICAN STUDENT, NO ONE HAS TAUGHT THEM TO YOU—BUT YOU NEED TO KNOW THEM FOR THE ACT.

As students write more in text message and read for the gist of a message instead of its technical content, they become further and further removed from the mechanics that govern meaning. Students have a tough time wrapping their brains around the idea that there are actual mechanical rules for writing, rules that go beyond punctuation and actually govern *how* to say things. Obviously those rules exist for clarity's sake, and one of the places they're most useful and easy to see is in the case of modifiers.

Modifiers are words that describe things—basically adjectives and adverbs. We use one-word modifiers, like *big* or *carefully* all the time, but we also use entire clauses and phrases as descriptors, too.

There are official rules about where we put those descriptors, and they're tested on every ACT.

1.–*ING* WORDS AND OTHER INTRODUCTORY CLAUSES

The easiest way to understand this rule is to see an example of the mistake in action. Check out the following sentence:

> *Leaping into the pond, the lily pads were perfect diving boards for the toads.*

Instead of just getting the gist of the sentence—of thinking, "Oh, I know what they mean"—you have to read a sentence carefully to derive its meaning from its structure. If you look carefully you'll see that in this particular sentence, *the lily pads* (which are plants) are doing the leaping into the pond, *not* the toads.

An appropriate edit for this type of question would be something like:

> *Leaping into the pond, the toads jumped from lily pads as though they were diving boards.*

To get a handle on the rule, tell yourself that whenever a sentence starts with a word that ends with –*ing*, like *leaping*, *talking*, or *weaving*, whoever is doing that action has to be be named directly after the comma of the modifying phrase.

Once you "get it," you begin to see how *any* descriptive material that begins a sentence needs to modify whatever comes directly after the comma.

Here's another mistake, this time without the *–ing*:

> *Considered the master of stained glass, Louis Comfort Tiffany's lamps are recognizable anywhere.*

This is a classic, extra-difficult sentence to edit, because it's easy to think we see the artist's name after the comma—but we don't. That apostrophe turns the name into the possessive, which changes everything: It's actually the *lamps* that are right after the comma. If you're rushing, it's an easy mistake to make. The sentence should be something more like this:

> *Considered the master of stained class, Louis Comfort Tiffany created lamps that are recognizable anywhere.*

That apostrophe/possessive is seemingly minor but it makes an enormous difference—and affects your score.

2. MODIFIERS: CLOSER IS BETTER

Another way to understand the technical rules of modifiers is by latching on to the idea that closer is better. In this next example, we don't have the introductory modifying clause as we just saw, but we do have some mix-ups that can and should be improved:

> *In the 1960s he began working on the concept*
> *for the screenplay, a decade of upheaval and*
> *social change in the United States.*

See how after the comma we have the words *a decade*? Those words are the start of a description of the 1960s specifically. In fact, if you look carefully, you'll see that in the sentence as it stands now *a decade* is describing *the screenplay*. We want to change that and put the *decade* stuff as close to the 1960s as we possibly can:

> *He began working on the concept for the*
> *screenplay in the 1960s, a decade of upheaval*
> *and social change in the United States.*

The ACT asks us to move single adjectives and adverbs, prepositional phrases, and sometimes whole clauses (as we just did) in order to perfect modifiers in sentences.

The most important thing to keep in mind about the English section is that there is a science to every question you encounter. When you look at the test, remember that probability and rules matter more than taste and preference. Know what you're getting into and you'll net points quickly.

THE MATH TEST

Overview: The ACT Math test is curriculum based and moves at a fast pace. It involves 60 questions that are solved in 60 minutes, and it covers everything from arithmetic and basic charts and graphs to some introductory trigonometry. Scoring is equally aggressive on the Math test. Make roughly 10 errors and your score drops down to around a 29; around 18 errors and scores drop to 25 or so. The questions on the Math section generally increase in difficulty. That doesn't mean that #34 is going to seem any more difficult than #33, but the material in the last 10 questions of the test will be significantly more difficult—or just involve basics from more advanced math classes that seem harder. We'll get to that in a bit.

Topics fall into 50 or 60 categories of questions, depending how you organize them. Yes, the ACT math is incredibly broad, but because the test is curriculum based—it tests straightforward things we see in school—a lot of what's on the math test feels immediately familiar to students. There is no way we could cover even most of the basics in Acing the ACT, so these obser-

vations about tricky questions are based on question styles that are peculiar to the ACT and, where we could fit them, those advanced fundamentals that most students need (re)training on.

———

STRATEGY ISN'T A GOOD STRATEGY. KNOWING MATH FUNDAMENTALS COLD IS.

Students wish that the convenience of strategy were a better way to prep—to their own detriment. Not only do students believe that test "strategy" (guessing, working backward, and so on) is of major importance to earning a top score on the Math section, they also tend to want to rely on it more than on developing connoisseurship of the test, learning the fundamentals, and growing their creative-thinking and problem-solving skills.

Guessing strategies as recommended by other test prep companies are theoretically designed to help students guess when they are stumped by a question but have some semblance of an idea of where the question is going. Personally, I've been in that situation maybe twice in ten years—I feel that if I am familiar enough with the question to know more or less what the answer should be, I'm actually familiar enough with the material to actually *quickly do the problem*.

While guessing is less of an issue on the ACT because there is no penalty for incorrect answers, trying to guess your way through and psychoanalyze the answer choices is just as time-consuming as simply doing the calculations.

This doesn't pay off—not on the ACT, and not in life, which matters a lot more.

Here's what's important to understand about the Math test:

1. "INFORMED GUESSING STRATEGIES" ARE BOGUS

Major test prep companies have popularized the idea that guessing strategies can and should be used on standardized tests as often as possible. The truth is a bit different. The informed, deductive guessing strategies popularized by these firms rely on a student having a fundamental understanding of the basics needed to solve a particular problem. Students use these basics to reason out what the answer should more or less look like because of their knowledge of basics. *Then* they use different theories about how incorrect multiple choice answers are constructed to suss out what the right answer might be.

I have a twofold problem with this: (1) The ACT is so heavily based on fundamentals that if you know the fundamentals well enough to reason through the problem, you know the fundamentals well enough to actually *do* the problem. You'd be better off just solving it and arriving at the right answer than messing around with guessing. (2) Test makers aren't from Mars. It's not as if they don't know all those guessing strategies themselves, and it's not as though the answer choices aren't constantly changed and rearranged to conspire against the use of those eliminative theories.

The bottom line is that students should learn as much math as they can and solve as much as they can as quickly and accurately as possible. That's what leads to top scores.

2. STUDENTS USE THE ANSWER CHOICES TOO MUCH—AND NOT ENOUGH

Students burn time reviewing answer choices. Students get all wrapped up in the answer choices, usually because they're trying to eliminate a choice or two before they actually begin the problem. They think they're saving time, but the truth is that this sort of reasoning to eliminate actually wastes time. Moreover, very rarely is a student equipped to winnow down choices to the best options without doing any work—work that would have just as easily led to the right answer quickly and easily without pseudo-analysis of the answer choices.

Students waste time by *not* having glanced at the answer choices, thereby doing too much calculation. You want to present answers in their expected form, so you need to know what that is ahead of time. The answer choices can—and should—guide you . . . to a degree. You'll always want to be aware of the following:

› Is the answer in decimals? Fractions?

› Does it include the root sign $\sqrt{}$? Is the radical simplified or not?

› Is pi written as π or did the answer get multiplied by 3.14?

› If we are presented with a trinomial or other polynomial, do we solve for the variable? Does everything cancel? How much factoring happens versus solving?

› If we're using the law of sines or the law of cosines (or even just the Pythagorean theorem or distance formula), do we solve for a real number value or do we just plug things in where they belong?

On a test that is as ruthlessly speeded as the ACT, no one can afford to accidentally calculate anything beyond what needs to be calculated. Know where you're going before you begin by glancing at the answers.

While it's usually safe to just solve a problem, some questions cannot be answered *without* looking at the answer choices. This is simple, but it stumps some people. When a question uses the language *which of the following . . .* , that language should serve as a direct suggestion to use the answer choices—not to come up with some inventive way of solving and seeing where it goes. The use of the phrase *which of the following* is indicative of the possibility of a myriad of answers, and so the test maker *has* to narrow it down for you with your answer choices.

3. "DIFFICULT" IS RELATIVE.

Here are three fast ways to think about strategizing your approach to math questions that would typically be categorized as the hardest on the test:

(a) Learn the trigonometry: Questions #45 to #50 aren't necessarily harder, they just test more advanced topics. In fact, they're usually very simple questions that simply reward students for knowing stuff that only a student who has taken Algebra II or Trig would know, even if that's just showing familiarity with a basic formula. We cover several of these topics starting on page 125.

(b) Topics you're unfamiliar with are likely going to be difficult, even if they're theoretically easy. Don't burn time on a question just because you've convinced yourself it's easy (because it's early in the test) if you really have no idea what's going on. Every question is worth the same amount of credit: Move forward! The next question might be far easier for you. Moreover, students forget that something they understand very well may be tucked in at the end of the test; make sure you see everything.

(c) Take a stab at the problem if it's about a familiar topic. Sometimes ACT "difficulty" isn't dictated by something "next-level" that students don't know; sometimes it merely involves multiple steps. Students brave enough to take a stab sometimes see where the question is going by simply following their noses.

WRITE DOWN ALL OF YOUR WORK—EVERY SINGLE DETAIL.

Students are doing work in their heads and making mistakes. So many students hate writing things down in math class. We all remember that one kid early on who never seemed to need to write down arithmetic and everyone thought he was so smart. Somewhere along the line "not writing anything down in math class" became synonymous with "the way smart people do math."

Breaking news: This just isn't true.

I'm taking the time to say this because I do not have a single student whom I do not have to constantly remind to write down the work. Even though they all make mistakes while doing math in their heads, they find it very hard to break the habit—if they're willing to at all.

Advising you to write down all of the work isn't micromanaging on my part; *it's strategic.* You want to think about writing down all of the work as a kind of insurance policy against stress on the test day. Remember that you won't be taking this test chilling out at your house in your socks while eating a bag of chips next to your cat Meatball. You're going to be sitting in a room full of super stressed-out teenagers who are all acting as though their lives depend on their ACT score.

There will be tapping, sighing, crashing around . . . and you, my friend, need to do everything possible to prevent yourself from making errors in a room of freaked-out people.

Writing down your work also lets you do one really sweet thing you could not otherwise do, and that is *check* your work. When you've written everything down, you can see what you did and review it. If you haven't written anything down, *you're not checking; you're redoing* the problem.

There is not enough time on the ACT to do every problem twice. There just isn't. Do the work on paper the first time.

Practice cross multiplication, please. For some mysterious reason, cross multiplication is on every ACT, and students screw it up constantly.

I don't want to make too much of this, but proportions appear frequently on the ACT (and in other problems I'm about to explain), and I've seen many advanced students not know how to solve them—sometimes merely because they haven't seen them in years.

So, here's a fast crash course:

First, while fractions are written $\frac{3}{4}$ in this book for typesetting purposes, you must write them vertically, numerator over denominator, like so: $\frac{3}{4}$. Doing so gives you valuable visual clues about where to go next.

Here's the mantra: if you have two fractions equal to each other, you cross multiply.

It is okay to cancel on the same side of the equation, but it is not okay to cross cancel.

Then you multiply: $\frac{A}{B} = \frac{C}{D}$ becomes AD=BC. An extremely common error is to think that $\frac{AD}{BC}$ is the result of cross multiplying. You'll see we lost the = sign entirely there, which is a disaster, because it's incorrect, and because you couldn't actually solve for anything when there isn't an equals sign. So, *cross multiplying yields two small multiplication expressions drawn from fractions that remain equal to each other.*

DON'T BE INTIMIDATED BY COMPLICATED ANSWER CHOICES.

Answer choices that look more complicated deter students from problems nearly identical to those they've already answered easily. It's not possible to get a perfect score on the Math section of the ACT without a reasonable understanding of the trigonometric ratios sine, cosine, and tangent. These are fairly universally taught using the SOHCAHTOA mnemonic [sin = opposite/hypotenuse; cos = adjacent/hypotenuse; and tan = opposite/adjacent]. Students should also know their inverses, cosecant, secant, and cotangent. (These all appear on the (M) card on page 125.)

Not only do we need to know what these ratios mean, but we also need to know how to use them in a variety of settings.

The most basic questions ask us to use these ratios to find the length of a particular side—and the result will be a simple number, like 9.2 or 8/7.

The exact same question will appear later in the test in disguise because its result retains the trigonometric expressions instead of calculating them. Most students look at the answer choices and think, "I have no idea," and skip them.

Let's take a look. One lower-level question might ask the following:

> In the right triangle shown below, which of the following statements is true about triangle ABC?

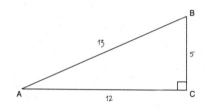

> F. cos B = 12/13
>
> G. sin A = 5/13
>
> H. cos A = 13/12
>
> J. tan A = 12/5
>
> K. tan C = 12/5

Now, any student familiar with SOHCAHTOA can find this result fairly easily by looking at the picture, figuring out the relationship of angle A's opposite side and hypotenuse to find that G is correct.

Here's the same question presented in a way that frightens most students:

> The instructions for assembling a tree house state that the ladder up to the tree house should be placed at an angle of 68 degrees relative to the level ground, which is perpendicular to the tree. Which of the following expressions involving cosine gives the distance, in feet, that the bottom of an 8-foot ladder should be placed away from the bottom edge of the tree in order to comply with the instructions?
>
> A. 8/cos 68
>
> B. 68 cos 90
>
> C. 8 cos 68
>
> D. tan 68/8
>
> E. 8 tan 68

Now, all we're going to do here is draw a triangle that would have been given to us in the previous, theoretically easier question. No problem! We draw a little sketch.

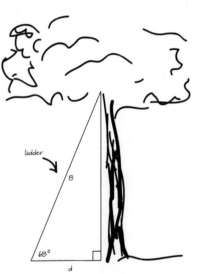

Then we set up the same relationship using the exact same SOHCAHTOA rules used in the last question and write down the relationship: cos 68 = d / 8. Rather than using our calculators to find the cosine of 68, we just imagine we're doing a cross multiplication problem to isolate d: $\frac{\cos 68}{1} = \frac{d}{8}$ and, voila, we find d = 8 cos 68, or answer C.

It *looks* fancy. It isn't.

KNOW THE ORDER OF OPERATIONS FOR PERCENTAGES: THEY HAVE SPECIAL RULES THAT MOST STUDENTS DON'T KNOW.

Stepwise percentage questions are designed in the hope that students will cut corners. A basic percentage problem simply creates a relationship between two things, a part and a whole, and shows what that relationship would be if it were proportional to 100. That's it:

$$\frac{part}{whole} = \frac{\%}{100}$$

There are usually one or two straight percent questions on the ACT, but often the test will include what I call a "stepwise" percent, which is a percentage question that, go figure, involves multiple steps.

> Tamar's time to commute to school increased by 20% from January to February and 10% from February to March due to traffic construction in her town. By what percent did her commute increase from January to March?

This type of question is very often a top-level question—and the last of the test. Most students respond by adding 20 and 10, saying the commute increases by 30 percent, and leaving it at that. That's where they get you.

It's always best to start solving this problem using 100—no matter if the question is about the price of hamburgers or telephones or a bus. When you start with 100 and work against that, you'll always arrive at an answer that's relative to 100, so it's already in percent form. That means time saved again for more difficult problems.

So, if Tamar's original commute was 100 (Minutes? Hours? Doesn't matter), when it increases by 20 percent we can say 20 is 20 percent of 100; so, 20 + 100 means it initially increases to 120. It's *that* number, the 120, that increases by ten percent the next month: $10/120 = x/100$ so $x = 12$. Add that 12 to 120 to find that her total commute increases to 132. We see, then, that her commute actually increases by 32 percent.

DON'T LET WEIGHTED AVERAGES AND FORCED PROBABILITY THROW YOU OFF COURSE.

Anyone can add up a bunch of test scores and divide by the number of tests to find the average score. Kids do it in school all the time in order to figure out their grades.

That's why such questions are virtually never on the ACT.

What *is* on the ACT, though, is a handful of average and probability problems that often trip up students. They're not actually far from what we see in school, but the way to solve them doesn't stick for most students, and that's why students get into a pickle on the ACT.

1. ADDING DATA TO AVERAGES: WHAT DOES THE NEXT TEST SCORE NEED TO BE?

It's very normal to see a question about forcing an average to become a particular value.

> To date a student has taken five 100-point tests and earned scores of 80, 86, 92, 88, and 70. What does the student need to earn on the sixth 100-point test in order to earn an average of 85 points?

So often a student will think she's going to plug in the answer choices, ostensibly doing five different average problems until she finds the one that works. On a test as quick-paced as the ACT, this is a poor strategy and costs time better spent on other, more challenging problems. Again, just because a question *can* be solved by plugging in doesn't mean that that's the best way to do it.

The best way to approach this problem is to do it algebraically. But even students who know this will go the wrong direction and fall into another time suck: they figure out the student's current average, which also has nothing to do with anything.

Instead, we should be *forcing* the average to become what we want it to be by using an algebraic equation:

$$\frac{(80 + 86 + 92 + 88 + 70 + x)}{6} = 85$$

where x represents the new score. That equation essentially says "these five test scores plus the new one, all divided by six, will force the average I need."

Solve:

$$\frac{416 + x}{6} = 85 \quad \rightarrow \quad 416 + x = 510 \quad \rightarrow \quad x = 510 - 416$$

$$x = 94$$

2. AVERAGES WHEN YOU DON'T KNOW INDIVIDUAL DATA POINTS

Another type of average problem tells you the average age/weight/score/whatever of a few groups of people and then asks you to identify the average (mean) across the group as a whole. It reads something like this:

> In the junior class at Douglas High School, the average GPA of the 400 female students is 3.7 and the average GPA of the 300 male students is 3.5. What is the average GPA across the entire junior class?

The typical reaction to this problem is to add 3.7 and 3.5 and divide by two, "since there are two groups," but that isn't the right calculation because there are more females than males in the class. The females' GPAs will weight the average, meaning there are more of them, so they'll skew the result. That's where students get stuck. What they usually don't understand is that it really doesn't matter if we know that individually Emily has a 3.8 and Patrice has a 3.6 and so-and-so has a 3.5. Because we know that their average score is a 3.7, it's perfectly acceptable to pretend for our purposes that they *all* have a 3.7. Moreover, we don't need to add 3.7 400 times; we just multiply 400 by 3.7 to get the sum of the girls' GPAs. Same for the boys: no one individual's score matters. We just multiply 3.5 by 300 to get the sum of their individual averages. We add those big sums and divide by 700, the *total* number of students in the class: $\frac{400(3.7)+300(3.5)}{700}$. That expression simplifies to show that the average GPA of all of the students is 3.61.

3. FORCING A PROBABILITY

While probability and average are not the same thing, the thought process that we use for a forced average (like in example 1, "Adding Data to Averages,") is the same as one used for a question of forced probability, and they have the same pitfalls, so it makes sense to look at forced probability here.

> A bag currently holds 10 marbles, 2 of which are purple and 8 of which are orange. How many purple marbles do we need to add to the bag to make the probability of drawing a purple marble from the bag ½?

Now, we've made this example simple, so you could theoretically use logic and counting to figure out how many purple marbles to add. The point here is to make sure you know *how to* use this process on less obvious problems.

First, probability is defined as the chances of success over all possible outcomes: $\frac{\text{success}}{\text{total outcomes}}$. That fraction can get dangerous: Here, we would define the current probability of drawing a purple marble with the fraction 2/10. Most students will reflexively reduce that fraction, and we do not want to reduce when we're dealing with probability. If you reduce, you *will not* get this question correct. We're dealing with the real, actual count of real marbles, and we're going to add more real marbles to that total count; reducing screws up the count.

Instead, what we're going to do is set up an algebraic equation that will use our existing count of marbles to force the probability we want.

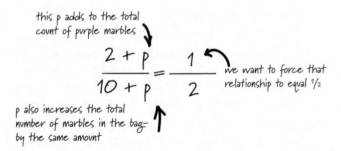

this p adds to the total count of purple marbles

$$\frac{2 + p}{10 + p} = \frac{1}{2}$$

we want to force that relationship to equal 1/2

p also increases the total number of marbles in the bag— by the same amount

Then, we cross multiply (as we often do on the ACT) and preform the algebra.

$$2(2+p) = 1(10+p)$$
$$4 + 2p = 10 + p$$
$$p = 6$$

So, we need to add 6 purple marbles to the bag to make the probability equal ½.

LOOK FOR HIDDEN DOUBLES. SOME ACT GEOMETRY PROBLEMS INCLUDE DECEPTIVE HIDDEN DOUBLES THAT ARE EASILY OVERLOOKED.

A particular kind of problem on the ACT involves the use of what I call "hidden doubles." These problems require basic geometry and arithmetic, but there's always a hidden division or multiplication element in the process and the vast majority of students overlook it.

A more basic example of this type of question uses rectangles to frame gardens or paintings.

> Jamal has a painting that is 18¼" wide by 12" tall. After he frames the painting, the width of the painting including the frame measures 22¾" wide by 16½" tall. What is the width of the frame that Jamal chose?
>
> F. 1¼"
> G. 2"
> H. 2¼"
> J. 2½"
> K. 4½"

Most students will subtract the width from the width or the height from the height and say the width of the frame is 4½". If we draw a picture, though, we'll see what we might be overlooking:

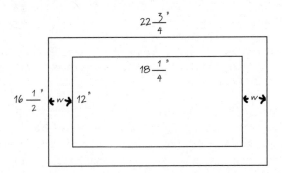

$22\frac{3}{4}$"

$18\frac{1}{4}$"

$16\frac{1}{2}$" ←w→ 12"

←w→

It's true that if we subtract the painting from the larger rectangle's length we'll get 4½", but that doesn't take into account that we're measuring the width of the frame *twice*.

We're actually saying 22¾ - 18¼ = 2w. Therefore, we have to divide that 4½ by 2 to find the actual width of the frame, 2¼". It's a hidden double.

Many students find this concept even less intuitive when we involve circles in hidden doubles questions. When the radius of a circle increases by 1, its diameter increases by 2, so it can be tricky to track. It's a perfect place for the test makers to sneak it in.

> A round pond that measures 54 feet in diameter sits in the middle of a field. During an especially rainy week, the pond's edge spreads outward

by 2 feet on Monday, 6 inches on Tuesday, and 1 foot on Thursday. What is the final diameter of the pond in feet after the rain?

More observant students will notice that this question is using feet and inches to measure the diameter of the circle. They'll presume that that's the tricky part of the question, and they'll convert the 6 inches into ½ foot, and then add 54 + 2 + ½ + 1, yielding 57½ feet . . . and their answer will be wrong.

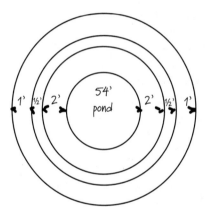

Since the pond is round, as its edge moves into the surrounding field, its *radius* is increasing, but we have to remember that it's growing in all directions, so it starts at 54 feet and then grows 2(2) + 2 (½) + 2(1), for a total of 61 feet in diameter. Again, the question is a hidden double.

THE KEY TO SOLVING MOST GEOMETRIC PROBLEMS BASED ON FORMS MADE UP OF MULTIPLE SHAPES IS MEASURING USING THE POINT WHERE THE SHAPES INTERSECT.

It's no secret that a radius is central to measuring a circle, no pun intended. The thing is, it's possible to draw a radius in two kinds of places in a geometric diagram: helpful places and not-so-helpful places.

The ACT people put the radius in the not-so-helpful places as much as possible.

Sometimes it's a little obvious. If we're given the radius of a circle like so:

we can't easily measure much about the square if the radius doesn't reference the square at all.

r measures the circle and the side of the square

If we slid that radius down, though, like this, now we see that not only does the radius measure the circle, but it also measures half the side of the square. The radius is a unit of measurement for *both*. That's what we look for on the ACT.

Here are a few other examples:

Below, the radius measures the circle and acts as a hypotenuse for a right triangle whose bottom leg measures the chord of the circle (thereby measuring half the length of the rectangle.)

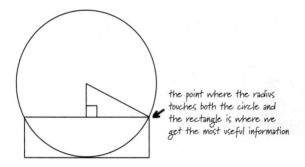

the point where the radius touches both the circle and the rectangle is where we get the most useful information

Below, the radius measures the circle and acts as the hypotenuse of a 30-60-90 triangle, which means we can measure the lengths of the legs of the equilateral triangle, too.

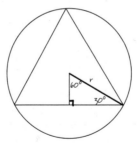

The same is true below; the radius just becomes the other leg of the 30-60-90 triangles.

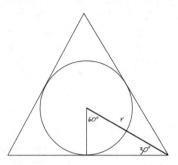

Remember, no matter what the case, the place where the two shapes intersect is the place where you'll get the most information for measuring both figures.

COUNTING DIAGONALS ACROSS FORMS AND GEOMETRIC SHAPES IS BEST DONE WITH A PROCESS RATHER THAN A FORMULA.

Students usually attempt counting problems by literally counting options. This is particularly difficult when questions ask students to count the numbers of diagonals in geometric figures that, of course, the ACT varies so that they are less predictable.

These questions will ask us to find the number of diagonals (lines through a figure that connect vertices), *sometimes between unconnected vertices (pegs on a board)* and *sometimes in enclosed figures (an octagon, etc.).* Because the ACT varies the forms, we need to know *how* to solve the problem. We can't simply memorize the formula.

8 vertices, 7 connections

8 vertices, 5 connections

You can see in the figures above that the number of diagonals is totally reliant on whether or not the shape is open or closed (rather than simply on the number of vertices, which is what we'd like to assume and what would make this question more formulaic). On the left we see 8 vertices with 7 diagonals; on the right, 8 vertices with 5 diagonals.

It's important to understand that diagonals by definition do not lie on the edges of shapes; they go *through* shapes.

We solve for the total number of diagonals by multiplying the number of vertices by the number of connections in each figure, but we can't stop there. There's another hidden double in this type of problem, as each of these diagonals has actually been counted twice in our multiplication problem.

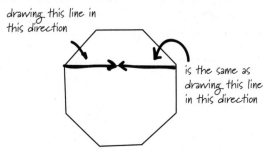

drawing this line in
this direction

is the same as
drawing this line
in this direction

so we divide by 2 to get rid of the doubles

We have to divide by 2 to find the right answer:

$$\frac{(\text{\# of vertices})(\text{\# of connections})}{2(\text{to get rid of the doubles})}$$

To wrap up our examples, then, if we solve for the diagonals in the peg picture, we would have (8 x 7)/2 = 28 diagonals. In the enclosed octagon, we find (8 x 5)/2 = 20 diagonals.

Always remember that the picture dictates *how* you'll calculate these problems.

THE DISTANCE FORMULA IS THE PYTHAGOREAN THEOREM, AND YOU SHOULD USE THE PYTHAGOREAN IN ITS PLACE WHENEVER POSSIBLE.

Using quick sketches and the Pythagorean theorem makes distance problems easier and increases confidence, which increases speed. It's like an insurance policy for your work.

It's easy to forget the distance formula (so many pluses and minuses!), but it's easy to remember the Pythagorean theorem. Many of the formulas needed on the ACT are related to the Pythagorean, and it's often simplest to apply the Pythagorean on distance questions for clarity and speed. Seriously.

If you remember the distance formula incorrectly and your alternative answer is a given choice, you'll likely choose it and get the answer wrong. With visual distance, you're sure.

> What is the distance on the coordinate plane between points A (0, 2) and B (1, 5)?

Rather than writing out the distance formula, draw a quick sketch of the points. Don't draw something fancy.

Just draw a quick, gestural plot of the two points more or less as they are related to each other, like this:

• (1, 5)

(2, 0)
•

Then draw the diagonal between them and two perpendicular legs attached to that diagonal so that it becomes the hypotenuse of a right triangle whose legs would be parallel to the x and y axes, like this:

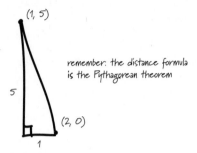

Now we're just going to use our common sense to measure those sides.

All we'll do is measure the lengths we've traveled in the x and y directions. In the x direction we travel from 1 to 2, so we're traveling a distance of 1, and in the y direction we travel from 0 to 5, so we label those sides of the triangle respectively.

Then we use the Pythagorean theorem ($a^2+b^2=c^2$) to solve $1^2 + 5^2 = c^2$. We could have used the distance formula to reach the same result, but had we made a computational error (or not remembered the formula at all, which is normal during a high-stakes test), it would have been difficult to detect the solution. Plus, for most students, this method is really faster.

$$c = \sqrt{26}$$

LOOK AT MEASURING IRREGULAR PERPENDICULAR POLYGONS LIKE A PUZZLE WITH SPECIFIC RULES.

There's a particular type of problem specific to the ACT that asks students to measure the perimeter of the shape. It looks familiar to students, but that's because they're often asked to "break up" similar shapes in geometry class in order to measure their *areas*.

They look something like this:

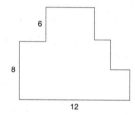

The difficulty level of these problems is entirely predicated on how many of those sides are labeled with their lengths. No matter what, you'll always solve a problem like this one the same way. There's no need to worry about the individual lengths of any of those legs: we need only to be able to measure the length of a *single* vertical side and *either* the top or bottom.

The simplest way to see and remember this (and to avoid obsessively trying to measure each side) is to think about this not as a formal math shape with drawn lines, but rather as a bunch of sticks laying on the table in front of you. All we're going to do is pick up those sticks individually and start moving them outward.

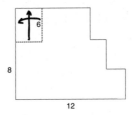

You'll do this for all of the "sticks" until you have what you'll see always turns out to be a rectangle:

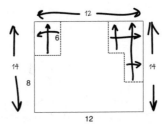

Since you know the bottom of that rectangle is length 12, so also the top must be length 12, even if you couldn't measure each of its component sides individually. Since the left side is equal to 14 (because it's 8 + 6), so also the right side must be equal to 14. To get the permimeter, all you do is add 12 + 12 + 14 + 14 and we have our perimeter: 52. Again, it doesn't matter if you know the lengths of the smaller individual sides or not.

Learn some basics of Algebra II and Trigonometry to gather quick, easy points throughout the ACT.

The ACT tests fundamentals of advanced math as a way of rewarding students who may have taken more advanced "college preparatory" courses. The ACT is designed to assess some form of "college readiness," and sometimes college "readiness" simply means "Yeah, I've seen that before."

This means that ACT test makers merely want to see that you have basic familiarity with advanced formulas from Algebra II and Trigonometry. You honestly need to just show the most fundamental understanding of these formulas. Many students don't realize this and lose valuable points because they haven't had a crash course on the formulas.

Seriously, whether you have taken these courses or not, learn the following formulas to earn valuable points just for knowing them.

1. CIRCLE FORMULA

You learn the formulas for area and perimeter of a circle early on, but the formula for plotting a circle on an xy-coordinate plane escapes most students after their last test on the subject.

First, you have to understand that the formula for plotting the edge of a circle on a coordinate plane, "graphing a circle," is just a jazzed-up version of the Pythagorean theorem.

$x^2 + y^2 = r^2$

It looks just like the Pythagorean, right? The only difference here is that the r value is the length of the radius and the x and y we're seeing are actually just an (x, y) pair that lies on the edge of the circle. This means that if you came across a circle formula written like the one above, perhaps $x^2 + y^2 = 25$, you'd know the circle would be centered at the origin with a radius of 5.

Now, the full version is a little more involved, but I want you to remember the Pythagorean when you're trying to remember where the + and − signs go in the formula. Getting confused on formulas is the worst, and rest assured the test makers will include all of the possible mistakes in the answer choices.

Here's the full circle formula as it appears on your (M) memorize page 131.

$$(x - h)^2 + (y - k)^2 = r^2$$

Now, all we've done is thrown in h and k. Notice that it's subtraction in there! In the circle formula, your h and k values represent the horizontal and vertical shift of the circle, respectively: They're the center of the circle. It's super important, though, to remember that the signs in the formula are opposite the signs of the actual center.

That means that if I see the formula $(x - 3)^2 + (y + 5)^2 = 25$, I am plotting a circle that has a center of (3, -5) with a radius of 5.

2. LAW OF SINES

The law of sines is just a proportional relationship between the angles and the lengths of the sides on a scalene triangle. Again, we'd use this formula when we are *not* working with a right triangle. Beware: Sometimes the test gives you this formula outright and sometimes it doesn't. Either way, if you know how to use a proportion and how to cross multiply (see page 57), you know how to plug in and use the law of sines.

The law of sines states that the relationship between the size of an angle and the length of its opposing side is proportionate to the relationship between either of the other angles and their opposing sides.

It's easiest to see in the formula

$$\frac{\sin A}{A} = \frac{\sin B}{B} = \frac{\sin C}{C}.$$

Now, of course when you're building a proportion you need only two values so that you can cross multiply. The rule just shows you can use any of the legs that you have.

Let's look at an example:

> Given the following triangle, what is the length of *BC*?

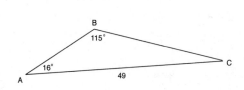

We're really just going to use what they've given us here to solve for the side opposite angle A.

$$\frac{\sin 115}{49} = \frac{\sin 16}{x}$$

$$49\sin16 = x\sin115$$

$$\frac{49\sin16}{\sin115} = x$$

Keep in mind that in order to make this more tricky, the given triangle may not be fully labeled, so you might need to solve for one of the angles in order to create a proportion you can use, but that's simple enough, as the sum of the interior angles of a triangle is 180 degrees.

Also, remember when we talked about how more complicated-looking answer choices deter students? These answers usually look very much like the example we saw there: You don't often need to solve for a value specifically. Rather your answer will be in the form of a fraction. Don't get scared when things look complicated!

3. LAW OF COSINES

The law of cosines is the law that scares students most frequently, and, coincidentally, it's also the one that you need to know the least about. While I can't make promises, I've never seen the test ever require that the law of cosines be used to actually *solve* for a value; you just have to know where parts go.

The easiest way to understand the law of cosines for our purposes is to think of it as vaguely related to the distance formula and the Pythagorean theorem. You'll be using this formula to find the length of a distance between two points (cities, islands, whatever), and you'll be using a scalene triangle to do so. The law of cosines uses a, b, and c, just like the Pythagorean theorem, and the distance you'll be calculating is c, just like the hypotenuse (which maybe you'll think of as the "important" part of a right triangle). Meanwhile, in this case a and b are interchangeable, again, just as in the Pythagorean.

Let's take a quick look at the formula:

$c^2 = a^2 + b^2 - 2ab(\cos c)$

Now, instead of just describing it, let's look at how that formula relates to a given scalene triangle. Just like on the other advanced basics questions, you're really responsible only for knowing what's what and who's who. There won't be any heavy lifting beyond that. Achieve a solid understanding of this, and you just might earn yourself another quick, easy point.

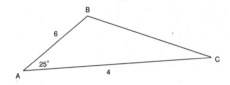

Using the law of cosines, what is the length of BC?

Again, I've never seen a question about law of cosines that required more than plugging in the correct values for *a*, *b*, and *c*, so that's what we'll do here.

Keep in mind that the length you're looking for is always *c*. In this case we'd plug in this:

$$c^2 = 4^2 + 6^2 - 2(4)(6)(\cos 25)$$

and then just root the *c*: $c = \sqrt{4^2 + 6^2 - 2(4)(6)(\cos 25)}$. The radical is what would appear in the answer choices, just as is. Law of cosines questions truly are answered just by plugging in.

THE READING TEST

Overview: The ACT Reading test is a 35-minute test that includes 4 passages: Prose Fiction, Social Science, Humanities, and Natural Science, always in that order. Each passage has 10 questions (for a total for 40 on the section) that focus on main idea, events in the passage, character perspectives, author meaning and intention, and finding specific details within the passage. We've heard that the double passages are coming, so be on the lookout for those, too. This works out to about 8½ minutes or so to read each passage or section and answer its corresponding questions.

Without an understanding of the Reading pacing versus scoring, many students cheat themselves out of top 10th percentile Reading scores.

The following breakdown from ACT.org shows percentiles for ACT reading scores, just to give you an idea of what raw score yields what. Generally, the rule of thumb is that you have to answer roughly 20 to 22 questions correctly to get a score of 20, around 26 to get a 25, 29 to 32 to get a 29, and 37 or 38 to get a 34.

Again, this isn't an exact science, but they're usable estimates. You should see from the above that, generally, if you get 3 of the 4 passages perfect plus a handful of extras, you'll earn a 29 or so.

Let me reiterate: 30 out of 40 questions correct on the reading section leads to a very solid score. It actually takes roughly 30 percent more work to earn a 36 than it takes to get that 29.

When students are not naturally fast readers but they don't qualify for extra time, we sometimes create an initial goal based on preset pacing: They spend 10 minutes on three of the passages and then 5 minutes on the final passage. The strategic idea is that they put in a very strong performance on those first three passages and then get what they can on the last passage to make up for mistakes or to tack on a couple of extra points.

Remember, you don't have to do the first three passages first; you can (and should) do whichever ones you tend to be most comfortable with, provided you're sure not to misbubble your answer sheet because you skip around. In fact, you could quickly skim the passages ahead of time and see which one has the most specific line references and save it for last, because, in theory, the one with the most line references should be the easiest to complete without really reading it.

The only way to know what score you're shooting for and to know how likely you are to get the answers right is to practice.

———

KNOW WHAT YOU'RE READING FOR.

Since you'll never know what passages will be on the ACT, it's wise to know what kinds of questions you'll be asked so that you'll know what to read for. It's hard to remember what the questions are if you read them before you read the passage, but if you go into the test knowing major question themes, you'll be far better off. The ACT usually asks the same sorts of questions. You'll be asked to make statements about:

› how *one character* thinks or feels about something happening in the passage.

› how *the narrator* thinks or feels about something happening in the passage.

› characterizing one of the people in the passage (commenting on what that person is like or how he behaves).

› the main point of a paragraph or groups of paragraphs.

› why things are happening in the passage, what may have happened in the past, or *why* people in the passage think or feel the way they do about something.

› why the author includes particular details (both as evidence and from a mechanical writing perspective).

› what the author or narrator means by using a specific word or phrase.

IT'S EASIER TO PROVE SOMETHING IS INCORRECT THAN TO PROVE SOMETHING ELSE IS ABSOLUTELY TRUE.

I've had students use a word-by-word process of elimination for years on the ACT with great results. It's not that process of elimination itself is particularly cutting edge, but the way we think about it is. I talk about how to approach standardized reading extensively in my book *Outsmarting the SAT*, so if you have a copy, that extended reading lesson is entirely applicable to the ACT as well.

I realized a long time ago that students internalize standardized reading tests as "tests of their ability to read," which really isn't the right way to think about them. They're really more tests of your ability to arrive at the same answer as the test maker— which is a test of your critical thinking and analytical skills.

To do that, we need to have strong critical thinking skills, and that means primarily analyzing the words that have been included in each answer choice to identify which individual words specifically are absolutely, completely incorrect. This is a much stronger version of the process of elimination that relies on the idea that it's far easier to prove that something is incorrect than to prove it's correct.

Many students initially balk at the idea of focusing on each word, but doing so has several benefits:

> It takes only one word to make an answer choice incorrect. Sometimes that word is *of* or *about*. If you're not thinking "every word counts," it's easy to overlook the small stuff.

> It makes a comparison between answer choices easier, because you'll be marking through words you *really* dislike. It'll be easy to knock out a few answers in the first place, at which point you can think very carefully about what the last couple of choices are really saying.

> Should you accidentally eliminate every answer choice, you'll be able to see exactly what you got rid of in each option. This sets you up to make a much better revision of your choices than if you'd crossed out complete phrases or crossed through only the letters that correspond with the choice.

> On the offhand chance you actually have time to check your work, crossing out word by word leaves a bit of a

"paper trail" for yourself of your decision making. You can see what you didn't like and what you went with in a matter of moments.

Practice eliminating word by word on every question you see, even on questions where you feel it's unnecessary. You want to train your brain to focus on individual words habitually, and the only way to do that is to do it *all the time*. Train as if you're taking the test.

Focus first on eliminating the most egregiously incorrect answer choices—those things that are clearly *very* wrong. Make a strong effort to cross out only one or two words within each choice rather than crossing out the letter of the choice or drawing long lines through the whole option so you can easily recheck your work.

As you work through your process of elimination, you may get to the point where you're waffling between two answer choices. In fact, I can pretty much guarantee that's going to happen. You have to remember that when you choose a final answer, you're saying, "Okay, I'm going to say B is right," and that means the other answer choice is incorrect.

Think about that for a second.

We're so habituated to look for right answers—we *want* right answers—that at the end we're more inclined to go for the one that seems right than to argue against the one that's *more wrong*. Meanwhile, choosing what's *more wrong and eliminating that creates confidence in your better, correct choice.*

Practicing eliminating word by word is all about building the habit of doing so, so that even if you're an excellent reader, on that handful of questions that you find tricky you will reflexively pick them apart and get to the correct answer more quickly and easily. We'll reveal more about what makes answer choices wrong coming up.

DON'T SELECT AN ANSWER JUST BECAUSE IT LOOKS FAMILIAR.

When students are in a rush, "I remember seeing something about that" is the go-to explanation for selecting an answer choice, and the test makers know it.

The ACT reading questions rely heavily on evidence, not conjecture. However, there are usually very few questions in each passage that cite specific line numbers; in fact, a big part of the initial reading strategy should be approaching the passages as though they are islands full of buried treasure (the treasure being evidence for the correctness or incorrectness of answer choices). Your goal is not to memorize everything in the passage but rather to create a mental treasure map for yourself as you read so you know where to go back and find topics and info as quickly as possible. That's why it's a great advantage to know what to read for in the first place.

For the overwhelming majority of students, not referring back to the passage while you answer questions is not an option.

Moreover, the test makers know that you'll be hoping to rely on your memory of what you read, as looking back can feel time-consuming, so phrases in parts of the answer choices may sound familiar. Parts of answer choices may be words lifted straight from the passage, so you know they're *from the passage*—but they're not the correct answer *to the question*.

1. THE PRIMARY PURPOSE

One of the most obvious applications of this tactic from the test maker is asking you to identify the main purpose of a paragraph and then including details from parts of the paragraph that are related to but are not its primary purpose in some of the answer choices. They can also do the same by asking about the primary purpose of the whole passage and then including an argument from one or two of the supporting paragraphs in the answer choices. Either way, it's most important to keep track of identifying the main idea, rather than selecting something that you definitely know you read but that was not central to the paragraph or passage.

2. THE HIDDEN DETAIL

You need to be aware that in each of the 10 questions on each passage there will be a question that refers specifically to *one* sentence in the passage. If you can't find that single sentence (or can't remember reading it), you can't answer that question. Because none of the questions are too theoretical (the test is too speeded to involve major literary analysis), one of the ways the test makers make perfection so difficult to attain is by asking questions about single details. Just be aware.

KNOW WHAT ABSOLUTES ARE AND USE THEM TACTICALLY TO ELIMINATE ENTIRE ANSWER CHOICES.

An absolute adjective is a great way to make something seemingly subjective absolute. One of the trickiest things for kids taking the ACT is remembering that even on questions that seem more involved or potentially subjective, the incorrect answers are absolutely, definitively, 100 percent wrong. Recognizing the strategic usefulness of absolutes is a first step to learning to think this way.

An adjective qualifies as an absolute when it describes a way of being that something either *is* or *isn't*. Take the word *perfect*, for example. It's a word for which there isn't any gray area: Something is either perfect—or it isn't. All it takes is one little blemish for something to be imperfect; there is no in-between, "kind of" perfect.

This sort of "yes or no" way of looking at adjectives is enormously helpful when analyzing answers because if the absolute adjective isn't correct, the whole answer choice has to go out the window. This should also reinforce just how important it is to read answer choices word by word.

Beware of the following words in answer choices and use them to help you make eliminations quickly:

> *Perfect*: Perhaps the character did something really well, but did she do it perfectly? (similar: *flawless*)

> *Original*: On the ACT, *original* means *the very first one*.

> *First*: First means *first*, as in something has never happened or been seen or thought of before. (similar: *began*, *initially*)

> *Only*: Only means *only*. Not a few, not "and one other time." (similar: *alone*)

> *Entire*: When we're talking about the *entire* thing, it means no other part of it is left out (so if Jane did the *entire* project, it means absolutely no one else helped). (similar: *whole*)

Pay special attention to chronology and past/present in passages.

Time-sensitive changes that happen in narratives should be primary points of interest. People change their opinions; they also change what they choose to do and say about a situation. These important changes occur in all four ACT reading passage categories.

ACT passages are often loaded with time-sensitive questions, and students often get these questions wrong. How could time-sensitive questions be so difficult?

The ACT is deceptively straightforward; so much of the way it tests critical thinking skills is through attention to detail. Paying attention to complex timing changes within a narrative can be particularly confusing, which makes these detail questions extremely challenging. When reading an ACT passage, it is imperative that you pay attention to changes in time, place, and opinion.

1. THE PASSAGE SWITCHES FROM PAST TO PRESENT

Occasionally a passage will switch setting midstream, but very often a passage—particularly the Prose Fiction and Humanities passages—will begin with reminiscence or explanation of the character's feelings or experiences that *happened* in the past and end with the author or character's *present thoughts* about those events. This might mean that little Susan is terrified of monsters at the start of the passage, but adult Susan doesn't believe they exist at the end of the passage. Characters could be vindicated, relieved, disappointed, hopeful—anything that involves evolution or change in perspective over time is common on the ACT.

This makes all the sense in the world: The perspective of a person as a child versus the person's perspective as an adult looking back in hindsight will obviously change, so it's a perfect venue for questions that require student specificity. These happen in the Social Science and Science sections when people in the passages—politicians, theorists, and scientists—change their opinions or expectations.

As you read the passages, be sure to underline any part in which you observe a change in perspectives or understanding of facts have changed.

Time-based questions that ask about this sort of thing:

> The author's (location, feelings, expectations) at the time of the author's (birth, illness, first public presentation)

> Public opinion at the time of the events in the story versus before the events began

> The initial feeling about something (in Science, this might be the scientists felt one way and then ultimately felt something else)

> The way the audience, society, or the author's family perceives something

> The revisionist interpretation of the data presented that was initially misunderstood

> Chronology

For this last sample, chronology, you might see something like: Considering the info given in the first three paragraphs, which of the following is the most accurate description of the author's childhood?

2. MOMENTS IN THE PASSAGE VERSUS THE OVERALL SENSE

These questions explore topics similar to those described previously, but they focus on feelings or perspectives at precise moments in the passage that may differ from the passage as a whole. They can be more challenging because they are less obvious, especially when a passage entirely focuses on one short moment in time (rather than a passage in which things overtly change).

While it's always important to go back and find evidence for the answer to a question—unless you are 100 percent sure you're correct—these are usually extremely specific and particular, so verifying your voice with evidence from the passage is a must.

We may read a passage in which a mother and father have a conversation about their feelings about a choice their son is making. Over the course of the conversation they both express different feelings, and those feelings might change. Then the test will ask a question like this:

> *Which of the following statements most accurately expresses Deborah's feelings when she hands her husband the cup of coffee?*

While we may have read about Deborah experiencing multiple feelings throughout the passage, this question has to be answered specifically. The line in which she hands her husband the coffee must be found, and her feeling *at that exact moment* is the answer to the question. It seems simple, but students get this wrong constantly because they either try to answer the question from memory and confuse different feelings at different moments, or worse, they can't find the particular action in the passage and have to guess.

THE SCIENCE TEST

___

Overview: The Science test is a 40-question, 35-minute science reasoning test that is meant to explore students' abilities to read and interpret graphs and charts, navigate basic science concepts, and think analytically about experimental procedure. It's best to have taken Earth Science, Biology, Chemistry, and Physics in order to have the easiest time with the Science section, but the section does not require memorization or knowledge of any formulas or scientific laws. Very rarely the Science test will ask a question that requires independent knowledge, but these instances are few and far between, and difficult to predict (and, if you're reading this, ACT people, they're decidedly unfair!).

The scoring on the Science section tends to be a bit unpredictable, too, and sometimes it's incredibly unforgiving.

There are only 40 questions on this section, and you can get only 6 to 8 wrong and still hang on to a score of 29. Missing 11 to 13 answers drops you down to a 25. To be honest, this is the section that usually drives students away from the ACT and toward the SAT. That being said, an enormous amount of patient

*practice can yield incredible results. I've seen student scores rise
from 19 to 29 on this section just by spending time with it and
getting an understanding of what they really need to know—and
what they don't—in order to answer the questions.*

———

A SCIENCE TEST THAT MOVES AT THIS RATE OF SPEED CAN'T POSSIBLY BE THAT DIFFICULT; IT'S DESIGNED TO BE DECEPTIVE BECAUSE OTHERWISE IT WOULD ACTUALLY BE *TOO* EASY AND STRAIGHTFORWARD.

The Science test is a basic test of scientific reasoning that uses specific methods to distract students from very straightforward answers. It always includes experiments about real, plausible topics; it won't be about the speed of rats on ice skates. While the specific topics might be unfamiliar to students, things will not behave unnaturally or against scientific principle on the Science test, so it's okay to make educated guesses around your general science understanding when necessary.

Moreover, this test is so speeded that it could never require incredibly complex analysis, even though at first glance it looks as though it covers serious physics, chemistry, and biology. Even though it appears tough, the answers have to be straightforward because they must be arrived at quickly.

In a sense, the only way for the test makers to make the Science test difficult is to make it really, *really* distracting and annoying. Here's a short field guide to the main ways the simple is made infuriating on the ACT Science.

WATCH FOR THE LABELS ON GRAPHS, BEING SURE TO CATCH THE DIFFERENCE BETWEEN TABLES, FIGURES, AND CHARTS.

Of course all of the graphs and charts on each experiment are numbered; we have to have a way of quickly and easily referencing them. However, they probably aren't labeled *quite* as intuitively as a student would expect. Consider the following: a question refers to Table 1. Most students reflexively scan for the numeral *1* instead of looking for the word *Table* or *Figure*. As it turns out, there's something on the experiment called Table 1 *and* something *else* labeled Figure 1. The student spends time poring over *Figure 1* when she should be looking at *Table 1*. This can easily cost a minute of precious time.

Tables, charts, and figures aren't only labeled according to which experiment they correspond to—they're labeled according to the order in which they appear.

STUDENTS ARE SOMETIMES ASKED TO THINK ABOUT SCIENTIFIC CONCEPTS THAT HAVE INVERSE RELATIONSHIPS, A PARTICULARLY CHALLENGING CONCEPT IN A SPEEDED SITUATION.

The ACT Science pointedly works against your intuition. Since the point of the science section is to test your reasoning, it is not suprising, then, that the test makers have researched ways to reliably mess with students' heads to make the act of reasoning that much more difficult.

The most common example we've seen involves purpose-fully confusing questions specifically about *density*. Think about density for a moment: when the density of a material increases, its molecules usually get closer together.

This happens in particular when gases cool: They slow down and move toward each other, thus occupying less space. Most ACT students know that. However, as the molecules are getting closer together, as the space they occupy *shrinks*, the density is *increasing*. In the midst of the ACT, students stop at contraction and shrinking, and are less inclined to say *anything* is increasing at all, even density.

As molecules cool, they draw closer together.
For most people, thinking about molecules cooling
gets them thinking along the lines of things decreasing . . .

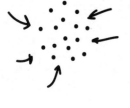

....but all that shrinking means that density INCREASES.

The overwhelming majority of students will overlook this counterintuitive relationship.

The same is true for pH. You're expected to know that we rank acids and bases on a scale of 0 to 14. As alkalinity increases, pH increases. Meanwhile, as acidity increases, pH *decreases*. Again, as acidity goes *up*, the *number* that measures it *drops*. That inverse relationship confuses students in a speeded science situation—so you're likely to come across it on the test.

EXPECT THAT GRAPHS AND CHARTS WILL BE LABELED IN WAYS INTENDED TO COMPLICATE OTHERWISE SIMPLE RELATIONSHIPS.

Graphs will be purposely designed to distract students by using words and concepts that make students flip-flop their understanding of what they perceive to be happening in the experiments. Since so many of the exercises on Science require simply reading graphs, the test makers more or less *have* to make those graphs convoluted. Otherwise they'd be testing grade school skills. Here's what to keep an eye out for:

A. RIGHT DATA TREND, WRONG PLACEMENT

You'll see graphs for answer choices that both illustrate the same trend in data, but one will be shifted up or down (or right or left), so if you're moving too quickly and look only at the trend of the graph and not at the corresponding numbers, you have a problem.

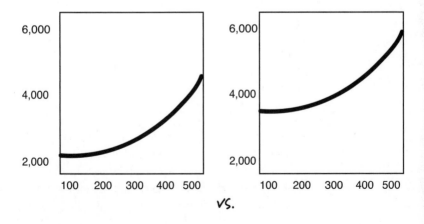

VS.

B. COORDINATE GRAPHS THAT DO NOT START AT (0, 0)

Since we intuitively think of plotted graphs on xy planes as beginning at $y = 0$ and $x = 0$, of course the ACT will plot values in which the origin is not at $(0, 0)$.

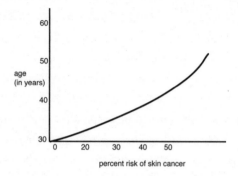

C. INVERSE THINKING SHOWS UP ON THE GRAPHS

First, graphs will use visuals and language that are designed to work against your intuition, just like density and pH are brought up in conceptual questions to confound you. In these graphs, things labeled *heavier* will be above things labeled *lighter*.

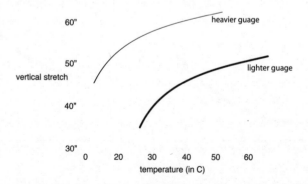

WHEN IN DOUBT, USE SEVENTH-GRADE SCIENTIFIC METHOD THINKING. RESIST THE URGE TO OVERCOMPLICATE THE ACT SCIENCE.

Dumbing it down to middle school science basics once you're accustomed to thinking about more advanced science is difficult and counterintuitive. There's an old aphorism, "*When you hear hoof beats, think horses, not zebras*". In other words, if you have any idea what's going on, think simple, not complex. Since this is a college admissions test, students are often guilty of expecting things to be far more involved than they actually are and they purposefully choose more complicated answers, thinking those answers sound "smarter." Your best bet is to expect simplicity and answer with simplicity.

When a question reads,

> *What is the reason that the students waited five minutes before reading the thermometer they placed it in the boiling liquid?*

you want an answer that basically says *because they wanted to make sure the thermometer had come up to the temperature of the water*—the same reason you'd wait a few minutes if you had a mercury thermometer under your tongue.

If the question says,

> *Why did the students wait until the fire had burned out completely before measuring the composition of the waste?*

you want an answer that says *they were waiting to make sure the reaction was complete.*

If a question suggests a change in the experiment, like,

> *Suppose the element being tested were dyed with green dye instead of blue dye. What change should the students make to their experimental process?*

you say, *well, obviously they need to change the colorimeter to read the new color instead of the old.*

The ACT always provides answers that sound extremely advanced in their explanations, and students are often tempted to choose these answers because they perceive that the ACT is testing "college level" material. Meanwhile, the simplest explanation is usually the best.

Extrapolation is allowed—don't be afraid of estimating beyond what the graph shows, when appropriate.

On the English section, we talked about how it's okay to add in new ideas and new words to the passages, provided that they're reasonable and they fit with what's already in the passage. This logic holds on the Science section, too. These questions are not particularly difficult, but students often feel as if they need permission to extrapolate, to read beyond the graph when the test asks them to.

It is entirely acceptable to extrapolate the trend of a curve beyond what you see in a given graph when the test instructs you to do so.

In the graph below, the data plotted stops at around 2008, showing a population of around 80,000 turtles. It's perfectly acceptable to say that in 2010 the turtle population will be around 85,000—or simply that it will be >80,000 at that time.

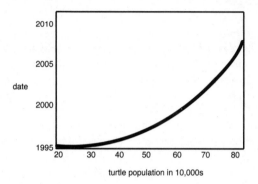

turtle population in 10,000s

"IT CANNOT BE DETERMINED" IS NOT A MIND GAME; IT'S JUST AN ANSWER CHOICE. SOMETIMES IT'S CORRECT, SOMETIMES NOT.

Students get into such mind games with themselves on tests, and the phrase "it cannot be determined" in the answer choices escalates those games to the nth degree. It is perfectly acceptable on the ACT to say that something cannot be determined when, in fact, it cannot be determined. Sometimes this is true because the data does not appear: The numbers aren't there, the boundaries don't appear on the graph, and so on. It's also the case that sometimes there is no apparent relationship between two groups of data.

It's just as valuable a scientific skill to know when there is no apparent relationship between data as it is to be able to articulate what the relationship is when there is one. Both are tested on the ACT. If the answer can't be determined, just go ahead and say so!

USUALLY THE FINAL QUESTION ON THE EXPERIMENT IS A BIT DIFFERENT THAN THE OTHERS, BRINGING IN NEW INFORMATION OR ASKING YOU TO DO WHAT SEEMS LIKE MORE ADVANCED REASONING.

The last question on any given experiment is usually the most hypothetical. Like everything on the ACT Science, the final questions are usually very straightforward but the general gist is hidden in as much wordiness and esoteric science as the ACT people can muster. I usually call them "more sugar in the cake" questions. A typical question will present the following line of thinking: *When Jane bakes a cake, she realizes through experimentation that the more sugar she adds to a cake recipe, the sweeter the cake becomes and the more people want to eat the cake. What would happen, then, if Jane added less sugar to the cake?* Well, obviously, the cake becomes less sweet and fewer people want to eat it. This isn't rocket science—but somehow, when we frame the exact same idea using technical-sounding science, students freak out.

In all seriousness, that's about as tough as these questions get. It's just that, instead, they'll be asking about 3 additional moles of NaCl in a solution resulting in increased salinity in an intravenous solution (or whatever), and then they'll ask what happens if there were 3 *fewer* moles.

There are two important things to remember about these questions: (1) They *are* far easier than they sound. If you read one of these and get confused, come back to it, because you're probably just brain-dead because the Science section is always last, anyway. Another pass later could clarify it. (2) If you *do* get stuck on them, remember that every question on the Science test is worth an equal number of points, so you don't want to burn time mulling it over when there are very likely much easier graph-based questions on the very next page. Circle it, guess, turn the page, and *move on with your life*. Please.

Students think they need to read every detail of every experiment in order to answer the questions.

Not only is it unnecessary to read all the given material on the Science section before answering the questions, it's also a waste of time. The Science test is a 35-minute test with 40 questions spread over 7 experiments. Moving quickly and developing a sense of pacing is of utmost importance.

Most passages will begin with a short introductory paragraph that tells you what the experiments are about. It's usually a good idea to read this so you get a sense of basic terms and the general gist of the experiments you'll see. Sometimes there will be an equation in this introductory material, too, and you'll want to take special notice of that. You don't have to take the time to understand it, but remember that it's there.

Each experiment usually has an explanatory paragraph that goes along with it as well. If you look carefully, you'll see that these paragraphs usually do little more than describe the data that appears in the charts and graphs. Rather than read these descriptions, you should spend a few moments looking over all of the charts and graphs, noticing the different elements they include. You'll comprehend the material more quickly this way, and you'll get the lay of the land for where to come back and find answer choices when you begin to answer questions.

You'll specifically want to notice the following:

› labels (Is this a chart? A figure? A graph? What are the labels on the axes? How many axes are there? Are there both a Chart 1 and a Figure 1?)

› units of measure (Take particular notice of weird and unfamiliar abbreviations or Greek letters because these will stand out in your memory.)

› when and where units and words appear repeatedly across tables and charts (This will help with cross referencing later.)

You'll want to forgo actually trying to make sense of any crazy diagrams that appear complicated and detailed—they may not even matter. All you want to do is get a sense of where to go back and find information and move on to the questions as quickly as possible.

THE READING-ONLY PASSAGE (THE ONE THAT APPEARS WITHOUT GRAPHS) IS INCREDIBLY ORGANIZED, SENTENCE FOR SENTENCE.

Very often there is a reading section in the Science test, a passage about experiments or hypotheses without any charts or graphs included. Everything you understand about the theories, experiments, and their results will come from the *reading*, not from any charts. We've never seen more than one of these questions on any given test, but they can be a bit time-consuming.

A typical example covers some background information that includes a bit of natural history and then a current scenario (maybe a lake has extremely high salinity or there's a giant crater in the ground). Then you're given two views about how that scenario came to be.

Here's what's important to remember about them:

› Go into these knowing ahead of time that the different points of view *could* be organized into charts and comparative lists. In fact, the explanations are usually written in almost perfect parallel structure, so if the first two sentences of one explanation are discussing the length of grass, the first two sentences of the other explanation will also discuss the length of grass. Similar topics won't be in the beginning of one but the end of the other. The separate explanations really do go toe-to-toe with ideas; if they didn't, it would be way too difficult to organize the ideas and analyze.

› It's typical to forget about the introductory overview—the narrative before the explanations. Sometimes proof of an answer choice will be buried in the intro—a date, an age, a chemical compound. Students ignore intro material in the same way they ignore introductions to books, so ACT test makers bury info there.

› You're reading for comparison of *other people's explanations*, not to draw your own conclusions about who is correct.

HOW TO SPEED UP YOUR PACE: YOUR PERSONAL PACING IS IMPORTANT AND SHOULD BE CALCULATED AND CALIBRATED. NOTE: YOU CAN ALSO USE THIS APPROACH FOR SPEEDING UP YOUR READING PERFORMANCE.

Let's make no bones about it: The pacing on Science in particular is incredibly unforgiving. This is one of those tests for which practice for pacing is important, especially if Science is not your strongest suit. You want to get a feel for how quickly you need to be working when you're in a timed situation long before you get into it.

If you, like most students, wrestle with the Science, you shouldn't just set a 35-minute timer, see how much you get done, find you haven't completed the section, and then freak out as your ongoing way of practicing. Doing so will be detrimental in multiple ways:

> › You won't be giving yourself time to think about the questions, so you won't be gaining a familiarity with their style and gist. In other words, you won't be developing connoisseurship of the test if you move too fast, so you won't get *better* at it, which is the point of the practice. If you *were* getting better at it, you'd get faster anyway, so you're shooting yourself in the foot.

> › You won't have any sense of how quickly you should or should not be moving because you'll simply be frantic, so you won't learn how to get faster incrementally.

When I have to coach a student to get through the Science test more quickly, I'll set him up with a timer counting upward. Then I'll ask him to work at a comfortable but steady pace so he doesn't feel frantic and can, instead, focus on getting right answers. I'll track his timing on each experiment individually, and then I'll sum those times to figure out what his natural working pace currently is.

Then, just like an athlete in training, you don't aim to shave 12 minutes off your next practice test. Maybe you shoot for 1 minute. You train yourself to relax a little bit more and move just a *hair* faster.

The beauty of doing this yourself is that you'll find that you actually *can* answer the questions on Science; you're probably just learning your way around the test and learning to analyze in the specific way the ACT Science wants. That can take real time. You'll also probably move more quickly than you otherwise would because you don't feel the pressure of the clock.

This is the approach we use to get students moving quickly and accurately over the long haul.

THE
ESSAY

Overview: The essay is an optional portion of the ACT test that comes after the four other sections—when you choose to take it. So many colleges require the ACT with Writing (the essay) that we absolutely have to talk about it. It's a 35-minute writing exercise that you'll write by hand, and like everything else on this test, it has some idiosyncrasies you need to be aware of.

It seems tough to strategize, to standardize, something as subjective as your personal writing, and that's why it's so important to go into an ACT testing situation knowing exactly what the readers are looking for. Every standardized test prioritizes something different when it tests writing, and the ACT is no different.

Of course the essay is going to require students to use proper grammar, to include multiparagraph structure, to use great vocabulary, and to vary their sentence structure. Moreover, you'll hear a lot of rumors about how essay length is a predictor of a high score, but I'd argue that's more correlative than causative: sure, longer essays probably get higher scores more frequently, but not because of their longer length—it's because of their better content.

Either way, "write a long essay" is pretty vague advice—probably not what you're looking for come test time. Rather than me pontificating about what I think is a super essay, let's check out the specific guidelines the ACT folks set forth. After all, if this is a standardized test, there have to be standardized rules for success.

Below are the qualifications for a top-scoring, perfect-6 essay. (Keep in mind that on both tests your essay is read by two graders, creating a possible score of 12).

The ACT essay, more than any other standardized test essay I've seen, values content above all.

According to *The Real ACT Prep Guide*, a perfect ACT essay response has these qualities:

› "represents strong responses to the writing task"

› "recognizes and addresses the complexity of the issue by dealing with several perspectives on the issue"

› "explores some cultural dimensions of the issue"

› "anticipates and responds to counterarguments"

› "organization is clear" and "transitions reflect the writer's logic"

› "introduction offers a full context for the issue"

› "language is effective"

› "good command: sentences are varied and word choice is varied and precise"

Let that sink in: The ACT essay is looking for your recognition of the complexity of the issue, for your ability to examine it from multiple sides, and for you to consider the cultural implications of the issue. The rest is just mechanics.

The ACT essay rewards creative/critical thinking and problem solving above all else. While you may think this is fantastic news because it sounds as if you're off the hook grammatically, don't celebrate too soon. First, your grammar and usage absolutely matters. English teachers are going to be reading your writing, so don't dare distract them with lousy mechanics. Fortunately, you'll have a solid grasp of decent grammar and mechanics because of the tips we saw in the English section.

Second, ACT essay prompts are not always so easy to expound on because they are often presented as A or B choices; they are questions that address *real life* situations or preferences—like creating parameters for teenagers to earn their driver's licenses or reducing tardiness in schools. If you don't show that you see the multiple layers of issues that these seemingly simple questions create (meaning you say, "Yes, grade point average is a great way to qualify teenagers for driving and this is why"), you're not going to earn a 6. You *might* earn a 5, but the 6 isn't happening.

The skill is to think beyond the A or B answer and, instead, show both complexity and solutions.

Here's an example: A typical question might ask you if students should be required to earn and maintain a 2.0 GPA in order to get a driver's license. In fact, it's the first example in the indispensable *The Real ACT Prep Guide*, which you should be using for practice material if you're prepping for the ACT.

Anyway, this 2.0 GPA question sounds very straightforward: Should we require a C average or not?

Now, remember, the ACT essay is all about nuance. An outstanding ACT essay is going to respond to the question with far more than a simple yes or no. Top ACT essays examine what I call the "meta-issue" or key point, that the essay addresses. Our driver's license question isn't really about how good one's grades should be in order to be permitted to drive; it's about how we make sure that everyone is safe on the road.

IDENTIFYING THAT KEY POINT, THE META-ISSUE AT HAND, IS THE KEY TO A 6 ON THE ACT ESSAY.

In response to the driver's license issue, an essay that earns a 6 would probably argue using the following points:

> It is common knowledge that teenagers are more likely to be in car accidents than any other age group, as evidenced by their unusually high insurance rates.

> Keeping teenagers safe in cars and encouraging safe driving among teenagers is of paramount importance.

> Indeed, supporting a rule that requires students to retain a specific grade point average may help weed out some dangerous drivers. However, teenage drivers should be put through rigorous driver's education and alcohol abuse education. They should also be put under a curfew until the age of 18, thereby further preventing late-night drinking, reckless driving, and drag racing.

> While further education against the dangers of speeding, alcohol abuse, and drag racing may not prevent all deaths,

these stronger rules and guidelines will certainly reduce teen driving fatalities more than a GPA standard alone.

Important to note: It's not unlikely that as a teenager you would never want to write an essay including the points I've just cited. Why? Because you probably don't want to advocate for stricter rules in a world where you may already feel pretty limited. Remember that when you're writing for the ACT, the side of the argument that you can most easily prove your point and expand your ideas is the side you want to write about, whether you like it or not. Often that'll be an argument that calls for you, the teenager, to be more responsible, driven, and reliable.

So be it.

Remember, the meta-issue is the issue that's really really at stake when the ACT proposes extending the school year or requiring a minimum GPA in order to qualify for a driver's license. These rules are not rules for their own sakes; they're actually intended to address something bigger: in the case of the extended school year, the rule ensures that students get a great education and have time to prepare for college, and in the drivers' license prompt, the rule attempts to keep teenagers—and all drivers—safe on the roads.

It's important to go into the ACT prepared with a general outline that you can use to help you think about framing and addressing the meta-issue on your ACT Writing test. With outline in mind, you can address the complexity of the issue and therefore write that fabled long, thorough essay that actually addresses what the prompt is really getting at.

This is not a formula that you absolutely have to stick to, but it can help you get in the habit of thinking like the ACT people want you to, and that's a good thing.

Here's the ACT.org explanation of what the prompt is going to do:

Prompts used for the ACT Writing test do the following:

> › describe an issue relevant to high school students
>
> › ask examinees to write about their perspective on the issue

"As a starting place, two different perspectives on the issue will be provided. Examinees may choose to support one of these perspectives or to develop a response based on their own perspective."

The final question the prompt asks is always going to sound like this:

> *Do you agree that students should be required to attend financial management classes while still in high school?*

No matter what topic they give you, your life will be easier—and they will reward you—if you explore the question at a deep level in light of the meta-issues. They don't need you to be too predictable in format, and you can get a 6 whether you write this in 5 paragraphs or 7. It's most important to show thorough thought; this outline aims to help you do that.

INTRODUCTORY SEGMENT (1 TO 2 PARAGRAPHS, DEPENDING HOW YOU FRAME IT)

1. Here's where you come in swinging. The ACT people love "critical context," which is why I'm obsessed with the meta-issue. Essentially, the meta-issue answers the most important question: *Why do we even care about this?!*

In your introduction you're going to mention the different perspectives presented and then *show you know what the question is really about*. This is how you show you understand the real context in which you're writing your response. You can do this in any order you like: lead with their examples and bring in your own or jump right in with a discussion of the meta-issue and then mention their ideas as not really addressing the big idea. At any rate, be clear that you know what we're really addressing is something like education, community safety, or healthy students. It's *never* just about the yes-or-no question.

2. Your intro should also be clear about your response to the question *in light of the meta-issue*. You can think of this as your thesis statement if that helps you. You may just agree with the prompt's way of addressing the issue (you might agree and say that a 3.0 requirement for extracurriculars makes sense), or you might actually evolve your response into your own more effective perspective or solution. What's most important is that you don't just devolve back into a yes-or-no stance.

For example, in *The Real ACT Study Guide*, the student who scores a 6 responds to a prompt asking whether we should have a school dress code by asserting that a dress code actually won't cut it. She suggests a more strict solution: uniforms.

BODY PARAGRAPHS

ACT body paragraphs have to make sense. Seriously. You have to be logical and sound as though you have real reasons (not inventive, far-fetched teenager reasons) for arguing the way you've chosen to.

There are a few ways to support your response to the question (your thesis statement) that can help you think broadly and write a thorough response.

1. APPROACH ONE: PERSPECTIVES

There are usually stakeholders who would be affected by your solution—people who care about the meta-issue in one way or another. I'm talking about parents, teachers, students, community members, coaches—these groups usually have some perspective on the solution you're proposing. It's totally fine for you to write a paragraph about how parents would benefit from your solution, how teachers would benefit, and even a third paragraph about your personal opinion. The student in *The Real ACT Prep Guide* writes this way, providing a strong response.

2. APPROACH TWO: RATIONALE

This is more or less the same approach as showing people's perspectives, but instead of talking about the people who care, you'll talk about three *solid and clearly different reasons* that your solution is a good one, three "whys." This is actually the trickiest one for most students, which is why I often say, when in doubt, use the perspectives format.

If you repeat yourself, you're going to seem as if you did not clearly think through the implications of the prompt, and English teachers hate repetition. You've been warned.

3. APPROACH THREE: THREE MINI SOLUTIONS

It's entirely possible that you will read the prompt and its pro-posed solution, and think the proposed solution is stupid. You'll know that the prompt is getting at something good—you'll really understand the meta-issue—and yet you'll still have a hard time coming up with something better and more brilliant than what they've already proposed. This is when you might want to use three mini solutions instead.

For example, you might think that the grade point average limitation for obtaining a driver's license is really bad, and that's fine—it's true that it's pretty arbitrary. But you're perceptive enough to know that what's really at issue is how to make sure teenagers that get driver's licenses are safe on the roads. In this case, you could write three body paragraphs that suggest ways to bolster safe driving: maybe an extended drivers' education course, a full license a year later than the current law allows, and curfews. Whatever. The point is, if you can't think of one big heroic solution and you're in a bind, come up with three little ones and always reinforce how they address the meta-issue.

No matter which avenue you choose, make sure you're using appropriate, supporting details. Be specific! The more specific your examples and reasons, the more believable they are.

THE COUNTERARGUMENT—INCLUDE IT!

This puts the "critical" in "critical context," which the ACT people love. If there's one thing you've probably figured out by now, it's that life isn't always so clear-cut. There are always going to be reasons, small and big, that your proposed solution to the meta-issue isn't going to absolutely, perfectly solve every problem the meta-issue causes. That's fine; that's real life.

It shows strength of thought for you to acknowledge possible weaknesses in the argument (i.e., yes, a high GPA doesn't guarantee you'll never get into a car accident, or, of course, kids will still find a way to compete with each other and show off style even if they're wearing uniforms). I have yet to see a perfect ACT essay that doesn't at the very least *allude* to a counterargument. Some do so in the introduction, but it's easiest to do it at the end, once you're crystal clear on the argument you've set forth and the strength of your examples.

It's best to include several sentences that explore the drawbacks of your solution

CONCLUSION

Wrap it up. Write a strong conclusion, but don't go crazy over it. A sentence or two will suffice if you're under time constraints. Most important, don't try to bring in new examples in your conclusion. As a structural element, the conclusion exists only to wrap things up, not to open up more ideas. Remember, though, that your strength is in your argument, so don't spend too much time on your conclusion at the expense of a strong introduction and body paragraphs.

THE MOST
IMPORTANT SECRET

This book is full of ACT secrets. I think they're special, and I'm proud of how they've helped so many students all over the world.

There is, however, one secret you won't often hear when you're prepping for the ACT, and I couldn't live with myself if I failed to share it with you.

Ready?

The ACT is not the most important thing.

Of course it's true that the ACT is a significant element of your college application, but you already know that. I want you to think bigger. I want you to understand that what should consume most of your attention in life is *living it*, and living it *well* as *early* on as you possibly can.

If you've read this book, you obviously have some measure of ambition. Perhaps you're shooting for the Ivy League or a special scholarship. I applaud your drive!

But remember, there are few things within your control that will help you advance over the course of your life more than developing resilience, enjoying working through challenges, and practicing kindness.

Life goes on. You'll win and lose, just like the rest of us. Bouncing back is defining. Learn to love tackling problems and remind yourself daily that we're all in this together, so be generous.

Best wishes for your success!

—Elizabeth

There are no tricks for questions that require these formulas.
Some things you just have to memorize, so you should know
these inside and out.

AREA AND PERIMETER

Know these basic geometric formulas for area and/or perimeter.

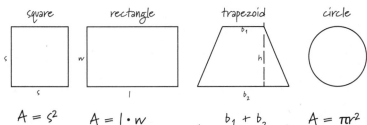

square

$A = s^2$
$P = 4s$

rectangle

$A = l \cdot w$
$P = 2l + 2w$

trapezoid

$A = \dfrac{b_1 + b_2}{2} \cdot h$

circle

$A = \pi r^2$
$C = 2\pi r$

TRIANGLE FORMULAS

Remember, the area of a triangle is always the same, no matter what its shape. The hypotenuse and height are always perpendicular to each other.

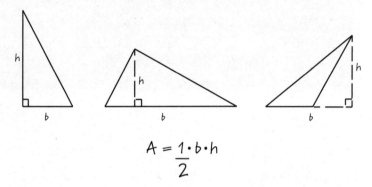

$$A = \frac{1}{2} \cdot b \cdot h$$

The lengths of the legs of a RIGHT triangle are found using the Pythagorean theorem, where c is always the hypotenuse.

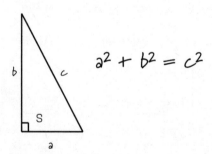

$$a^2 + b^2 = c^2$$

SPECIAL TRIANGLES

Recognize and know how to use these special triangles.

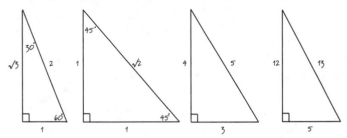

INTERIOR ANGLES

The sum of the interior angles of any shape
= (# of sides - 2) (180°).

Triangles have 180° and all quadrilaterals and circles
have 360°.

LINEAR EQUATIONS

A "linear equation" is the official name for the equation
of a line

$$y = mx + b$$

where m is the slope and b is the y-intercept

The slope m between any two points is:

$$m = \frac{y_2 - y_1}{x_2 - x_1}$$

DIFFERENCE OF PERFECT SQUARES

$x^2 - y^2$, the difference of perfect squares, always factors into

$$(x + y)(x - y)$$

VOLUME

Know the volume of these three-dimensional figures.

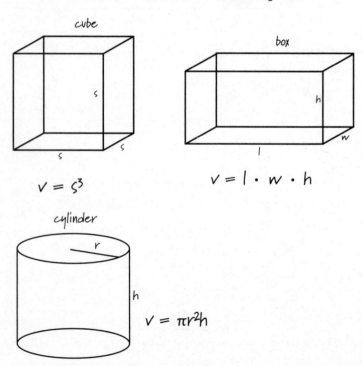

cube

s

s s

$v = s^3$

box

h

l w

$v = l \cdot w \cdot h$

cylinder

r

h

$v = \pi r^2 h$

SURFACE AREA

The surface area of three-dimensional figures is

the sum of the areas of each individual face of a form.

SINE, COSINE, TANGENT

Understand the sine, cosine, and tangent ratios and their inverses, cosecant, secant, and cotangent, respectively (the mnemonic SOH CAH TOA is useful here).

$$\sin = \frac{opposite}{hypotenuse} \qquad \cos = \frac{adjacent}{hypotenuse} \qquad \tan = \frac{opposite}{adjacent}$$

$$\csc = \frac{hypotenuse}{opposite} \qquad \sec = \frac{hypotenuse}{adjacent} \qquad \cot = \frac{adjacent}{opposite}$$

Also know this additional trigonometry

$$\tan = \frac{\sin}{\cos} \qquad and \qquad \sin^2 X + \cos^2 X = 1$$

For the graphs of sine and cosine waves

$$y = a \sin x + k \text{ or } y = a \cos x + k$$

a is the amplitude and k is the vertical shift.

EX: $y = (\sin x)$

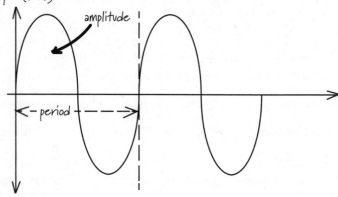
amplitude

period

EX: $y = (\sin x) + 2$

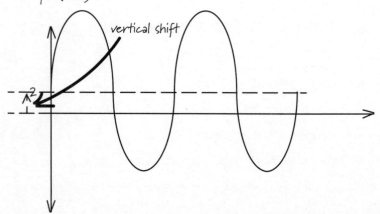
vertical shift

2

PARABOLAS

The formula for a parabola is

$$y = a(x-h)^2 + k$$

where (h, k) is the vertex. If a is positive, it faces up. If a is negative, it faces down. The bigger the absolute value of a, the narrower the parabola.

EX: $y = (x + 3)^2 + 2$ EX: $y = 2(x + 3)^2 + 2$

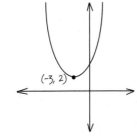 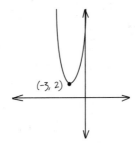

CIRCLES AND ELLIPSES

A circle is plotted on the coordinate plane using this formula

$$(x - h)^2 + (y - k)^2 = r^2$$

where (h, k) is the center of the circle.

EX: $(x + 3)^2 + (y - 2)^2 = 16$

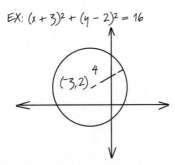

CIRCLES AND ELLIPSES CONTINUED

An ellipse echoes the formula for a circle

$$\frac{(x - h)^2}{a^2} + \frac{(y - k)^2}{b^2} = 1$$

where a and b are the lengths of its major and minor axes.

EX: $\dfrac{(x + 3)^2}{25} + \dfrac{(y - 2)^2}{9} = 1$

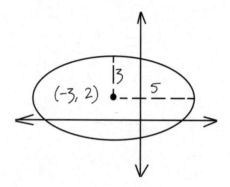

OTHER TIPS

Rather than memorizing the distance and midpoint formulas, plot the points and measure on a coordinate plane to ensure your accuracy.

Use Pythagorean theorem for distance, and vertical and horizontal shift for midpoint (see page 74).

© Lynn Parks

ABOUT THE AUTHOR

Elizabeth King is a teacher, speaker, and author of the definitive SAT prep book, *Outsmarting the SAT*, and the provocative culture and arts blog *Stay Out of School*. She is founder and president of the online boutique test prep firm Think Tank Education International, Inc., and the nonprofit organization Agency for Emerging Voices, Inc. Find her at elizabethonline.com.

INDEX